New Canaan Library

151 Main Street
New Canaan, CT 06840

(203) 594-5000
www.newcanaanlibrary.org

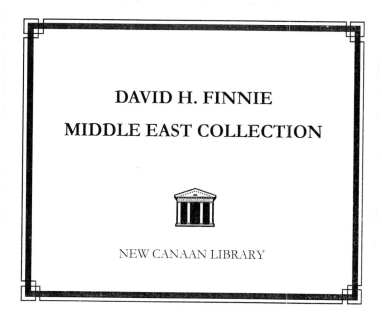

DAVID H. FINNIE

MIDDLE EAST COLLECTION

NEW CANAAN LIBRARY

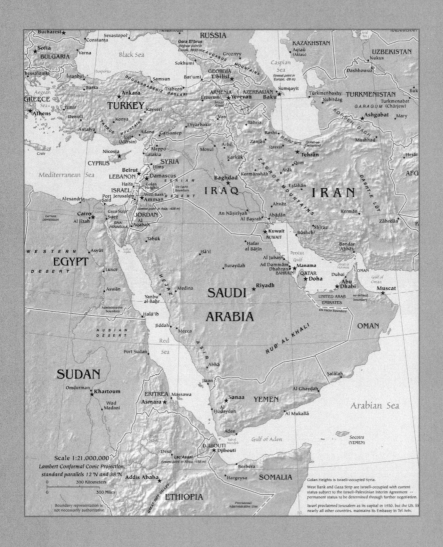

ARBITRARY BORDERS

Political Boundaries in World History

The Division of the Middle East
The Treaty of Sèvres

Heather Lehr Wagner

Foreword by
Senator George J. Mitchell

Introduction by
James I. Matray
California State University, Chico

CHELSEA HOUSE
PUBLISHERS
A Haights Cross Communications Company

Philadelphia

FRONTIS   Map of the Middle East Region.

CHELSEA HOUSE PUBLISHERS

VP, NEW PRODUCT DEVELOPMENT   Sally Cheney
DIRECTOR OF PRODUCTION   Kim Shinners
CREATIVE MANAGER   Takeshi Takahashi
MANUFACTURING MANAGER   Diann Grasse

Staff for THE DIVISION OF THE MIDDLE EAST

EXECUTIVE EDITOR   Lee Marcott
PRODUCTION EDITOR   Megan Emery
ASSISTANT PHOTO EDITOR   Noelle Nardone
INTERIOR DESIGN   Keith Trego
COVER DESIGNER   Keith Trego
LAYOUT   EJB Publishing Services

Contents

Foreword

Senator **George J. Mitchell**

I spent years working for peace in Northern Ireland and in the Middle East. I also made many visits to the Balkans during the long and violent conflict there.

Each of the three areas is unique; so is each conflict. But there are also some similarities: in each, there are differences over religion, national identity, and territory.

Deep religious differences that lead to murderous hostility are common in human history. Competing aspirations involving national identity are more recent occurrences, but often have been just as deadly.

Territorial disputes—two or more people claiming the same land—are as old as humankind. Almost without exception, such disputes have been a factor in recent conflicts. It is impossible to calculate the extent to which the demand for land—as opposed to religion, national identity, or other factors— figures in the motivation of people caught up in conflict. In my experience it is a substantial factor that has played a role in each of the three conflicts mentioned above.

In Northern Ireland and the Middle East, the location of the border was a major factor in igniting and sustaining the conflict. And it is memorialized in a dramatic and visible way: through the construction of large walls whose purpose is to physically separate the two communities.

In Belfast, the capital and largest city in Northern Ireland, the so-called "Peace Line" cuts through the heart of the city, right across urban streets. Up to thirty feet high in places, topped with barbed wire in others, it is an ugly reminder of the duration and intensity of the conflict.

In the Middle East, as I write these words, the government of Israel has embarked on a huge and controversial effort to construct a security fence roughly along the line that separates Israel from the West Bank.

Having served a tour of duty with the U.S. Army in Berlin, which was once the site of the best known of modern walls, I am skeptical of their long-term value, although they often serve short-term needs. But it cannot be said that such structures represent a new idea. Ancient China built the Great Wall to deter nomadic Mongol tribes from attacking its population.

In much the same way, other early societies established boundaries and fortified them militarily to achieve the goal of self-protection. Borders always have separated people. Indeed, that is their purpose.

This series of books examines the important and timely issue of the significance of arbitrary borders in history. Each volume focuses attention on a territorial division, but the analytical approach is more comprehensive. These studies describe arbitrary borders as places where people interact differently from the way they would if the boundary did not exist. This pattern is especially pronounced where there is no geographic reason for the boundary and no history recognizing its legitimacy. Even though many borders have been defined without legal precision, governments frequently have provided vigorous monitoring and military defense for them.

This series will show how the migration of people and exchange of goods almost always work to undermine the separation that borders seek to maintain. The continuing evolution of a European community provides a contemporary example illustrating this point, most obviously with the adoption of a single currency. Moreover, even former Soviet bloc nations have eliminated barriers to economic and political integration.

Globalization has emerged as one of the most powerful forces in international affairs during the twenty-first century. Not only have markets for the exchange of goods and services become genuinely worldwide, but instant communication and sharing of information have shattered old barriers separating people. Some scholars even argue that globalization has made the entire concept of a territorial nation-state irrelevant. Although the assertion is certainly premature and probably wrong, it highlights the importance of recognizing how borders often have reflected and affirmed the cultural, ethnic, or linguistic perimeters that define a people or a country.

Since the Cold War ended, competition over resources or a variety of interests threaten boundaries more than ever, resulting in contentious interaction, conflict, adaptation, and intermixture. How people define their borders is also a factor in determining how events develop in the surrounding region. This series will provide detailed descriptions of selected arbitrary borders in history with the objective of providing insights on how artificial boundaries separating people will influence international affairs during the next century.

Senator George J. Mitchell
October 2003

Introduction

James I. Matray
California State University, Chico

Throughout history, borders have separated people. Scholars have devoted considerable attention to assessing the significance and impact of territorial boundaries on the course of human history, explaining how they often have been sources of controversy and conflict. In the modern age, the rise of nation-states in Europe created the need for governments to negotiate treaties to confirm boundary lines that periodically changed as a consequence of wars and revolutions. European expansion in the nineteenth century imposed new borders on Africa and Asia. Many native peoples viewed these boundaries as arbitrary and, after independence, continued to contest their legitimacy. At the end of both world wars in the twentieth century, world leaders drew artificial and impermanent lines separating assorted people around the globe. Borders certainly are among the most important factors that have influenced the development of world affairs.

Chelsea House Publishers decided to publish a collection of books looking at arbitrary borders in history in response to the revival of the nuclear crisis in North Korea in October 2002. Recent tensions on the Korean peninsula are a direct consequence of the partitioning of Korea at the 38th parallel after World War II. Other nations in the course of human history have suffered due to similar artificial divisions. The reasons for establishing arbitrary borders have differed, but usually arise from either domestic or international factors and are often a combination of both. In the case of Korea, it was the United States and the Soviet Union who decided in August 1945 to partition the country at the 38th parallel. Ostensibly, the purpose was to facilitate the acceptance of the surrender of Japanese forces at the end of World War II. However, historians have presented persuasive evidence that a political contest existed inside Korea to decide the future of the nation after forty years of Japanese colonial rule. Therefore, Korea's division at the 38th parallel was an artificial boundary that symbolized the split among the Korean people about the nation's destiny. On the right were conservative landowners who had closely aligned with the Japanese, many of whom were outright collaborators. On the left, there were far more individuals who favored revolutionary change. In fact, Communists provided the leadership and direction for the independence movement inside Korea from the 1920s until the end of World War II. After 1945, two Koreas emerged that reflected these divergent ideologies. But the Korean people have never accepted the legitimacy or permanence of the division imposed by foreign powers.

Korea's experience in dealing with the artificial division of its country may well be unique, but it is not without historical parallels. The first set of books in this series on arbitrary borders examines six key chapters in human history. One volume will look at the history of the 38th parallel in Korea. Other volumes will provide description and analysis of the division of the Middle East after World War I; the Cold War as symbolized by the Iron Curtain in Central Europe; the United States.-Mexico Border; the 17th parallel in Vietnam, and the Mason-Dixon Line. Future books will address the Great Wall in China, Northern Ireland's border, and the Green Line in Israel. Admittedly, there are many significant differences between these boundaries, but these books will cover as many common themes as possible. In so doing, each will help readers conceptualize how factors such as colonialism, culture, and economics determine the nature of contact between people along these borders. Although globalization has emerged as a powerful force working against the creation and maintenance of lines separating people, boundaries are not likely to disappear as factors with a continuing influence on world events. This series of books will provide insights about the impact of arbitrary borders on human history and how such borders continue to shape the modern world.

James I. Matray
Chico, California
November 2003

1

A Meeting in London

On the morning of February 12, 1920, a conference began at 10 Downing Street in London, the home of the British prime minister, David Lloyd George. World War I had ended, and representatives of the Allied powers had gathered to prepare the terms of peace to be signed with the defeated Ottoman Empire, which had sided with Germany in the war. Previous attempts to resolve the terms for the Ottoman Empire (whose territory stretched from Turkey into Asia and included the Middle East and Arabia) had proved unsuccessful, and the question of how best to administer these territories had been left unresolved when the Paris Peace Conference concluded on January 21, 1920.

The Allies gathered again in February to attempt to resolve the disposition of the Ottoman Empire. Great Britain and France were interested in gaining control of the oil-rich, strategically important territories in the Middle East. In addition, Greece wanted to recapture Turkish-held territory in Anatolia.

On the morning of February 12, 1920, the first Conference of London began. There were no representatives from the United States—President Woodrow Wilson had been unable to persuade the Senate to ratify the peace treaty with Germany. Instead, those present during the weeks of meetings included Lloyd George; the British secretary of state for foreign affairs, Earl George Curzon; the French premier, Alexandre Millerand; Italy's prime minister, Francesco Nitti; their secretaries and an interpreter; and, on occasion, the Japanese ambassador and representatives from Greece, Belgium, and Romania.

On the first day, the principals all noted the difficulties they had experienced in finding time to attend these meetings. Millerand expressed his hope that the conference could be kept short, as it was difficult for him to remain away from France for an extended period of time. Lloyd George quickly responded that Monsieur Millerand could now appreciate how difficult it had been for him to stay in Paris for seven months the previous year (for the Paris Peace Conference).[1] Nitti noted that he, too, found it difficult to be away from his country for an extended

British Prime Minister David Lloyd George played an important role in the discussions of how best to administer the break–up of the Ottoman Empire. He supported the dismantling of the empire and its assets, as well as Allied occupation of Turkish territories.

period of time. He reminded his colleagues that their focus should be on achieving "a definite and durable peace."[2] Lloyd George responded that he agreed that peace should be the ultimate goal, but if they were not even able to agree on where the peace conference would be held, it was unlikely that they would be able to agree on a unified plan for peace.[3]

By February 14, the Allied leaders' attention had shifted to the terms of peace with Turkey. Great Britain, France, and Italy were in agreement on six basic principles: (1) that an independent Turkish state should be maintained in some form; (2) that international control should be established in the Dardanelles and Bosporus; (3) that Turkey's military should be reduced or disbanded to prevent it from threatening the peace; (4) that the Allies were committed to establishing an independent Armenia; (5) that Syria, Mesopotamia (now known as Iraq), and Palestine (the territory now making up the nations of Israel and Jordan) should all be separated from Turkey; and (6) that Christian minorities in Turkey must be protected.

From these basic points of agreement, many questions arose. Turkey was at that time ruled by a sultan in Constantinople (also known as Istanbul). Would he remain in power, and, if so, precisely how much power would he retain? If the size of the Turkish military were to be reduced, precisely what kind and size of force would remain? Would Turkish territory be given to Greece, and, if so, how much? Greece had already seized Smyrna. Could that occupation continue, and, if so, for how long?

The central question remained whether any size or form of independent Turkish state would be allowed to exist. Turkey had incurred substantial debt before the war, and now that the war had ended, war expenses plus claims for reparations had added to these debts.

Religion was also a concern, one voiced by the French premier, who noted that France's Muslim population would watch carefully the treatment of the sultan in Constantinople (who also served as *caliph*, the Islamic religious leader). The Italian prime minister suggested that the sultan in Constantinople should be retained to serve as a spiritual leader, much as the pope governed the Catholic Church from the Vatican.

The largest Islamic empire in the world at the time of the London Conference was the British Empire. It would have been expected that Prime Minister Lloyd George would carefully weigh his words, noting the impact of his comments not merely in

Turkey but throughout the empire. He did not agree with Prime Minister Nitti that the sultan should remain in Constantinople to prevent unrest among Muslims, however. In fact, he suggested that all Turks should be forced out of their capital city.

The Turk, Lloyd George noted, had been in Europe for hundreds of years and was always "a curse, an oppressor.... We might now really be missing a great opportunity of ridding Europe once and for all of this pest and potential source of trouble," he said.[4]

Later meetings showed no softening of Lloyd George's disdainful attitude toward the remnants of the Ottoman Empire. The problem of the occupation of Smyrna by Greek forces—a source of intense anger on the part of the Turks—was raised by France's Millerand, who noted that British and French occupation of territories had proved less problematic to the Turks, and perhaps a compromise might be reached wherein the Greeks could be persuaded to move out of the occupied territory.

With this Lloyd George once again disagreed, arguing that asking the Greeks to move out of Smyrna would humiliate them and cause the port city to suffer. He noted that he might be willing to compromise on Constantinople, which would allow the Turks to remain in their capital city, but he saw no point in handing Smyrna back to "a people who had shown themselves utterly incapable of governing."[5] Besides, Lloyd George continued, whatever was done, the Turks would be troublesome, and "any idea that they won't give trouble in the future is absolutely futile."[6]

A ROTTEN EMPIRE

As the debates continued, these Allied leaders agreed that Turkey—the "fundamentally rotten empire," in Lloyd George's words[7]—must be expected to pay its war debts and reimburse the Allies for the expense of maintaining their troops on Turkish soil, to occupy its land and administer its people. Greece would be left to occupy the Turkish territories of Smyrna and western Anatolia for five years, at which point a vote would be held to determine whether the territories would become part of Greece.

Constantinople and the Dardanelles would be placed under international control. Armenia would be given its independence. Kurdistan would be given autonomy. The Turkish army would be reduced to no more than 50,000 men. The Turkish navy and air force would be disbanded. The Turkish economy—particularly the ability to impose taxes—would be under British, French, and Italian supervision.

Piece by piece, the Ottoman Empire was sliced apart, its fate settled by leaders thousands of miles away. Turkey was becoming a nonentity, its sultan a puppet for others to control. The borders that had once marked the beginning and end of the mighty Ottoman Empire were gone, replaced by arbitrary borders placed where they might most benefit the Allied leaders.

By February 27, 1920, the Allied leaders believed progress had been made. They turned their attention to the question of which nations would be allowed to sign the peace treaty with Turkey and to ways to address postwar economic difficulties in their respective countries. "Peace is not yet established in the minds of the people," Prime Minister Nitti commented, "and without peace there can be no confidence."[8]

Within 24 hours, the foreign secretaries and ambassadors met to discuss a very different topic. A report had been published in *The Times* stating that French troops had been forced to evacuate the territory of Cilicia (in Armenia) following an attack by Turkish Nationalist forces. The article suggested that thousands of Armenians had been murdered after the departure of the French troops.

The Turkish Nationalist forces were thought to be operating under the leadership of a former Ottoman officer, Mustafa Kemal. At first, the Allies sent messages to the sultan to demand that he control Kemal and force the Nationalist forces to disband. The helpless sultan could no more control Kemal, however, than he could prevent his people from realizing that their country was still at war. The meetings in London were determining how to bring an end to their nation, to their way of life, and to their right to determine their own future.

Mustafa Kemal came into prominence as the leader of the Turkish Nationalist forces at about the time this photograph was taken in 1920. He was to become the most influential figure in modern Turkish history and is considered the founder of modern Turkey.

The Allied leaders continued their meetings and ultimately authorized the British occupation of Constantinople to bring the Nationalist forces under control. They believed that their decisions and actions—the borders they were placing where none had existed before—would cement their positions in Turkey and the Middle East and transform the region forever.

In the end, these statesmen would transform the world, although not in the way they imagined. As they debated from a distance about where the borders of Turkey would begin and end, how it would be governed, and who its people would be, a revolution was already taking place that would settle these very questions. Its leader was Mustafa Kemal, who had his own vision of Turkey—a strong, independent, European Turkey— and was determined to inspire his countrymen to help him turn this vision into reality. The military superiority of the British and French, the realities of the Allied occupation, were merely obstacles to overcome.

"A nation must be strong in spirit, knowledge, science and morals," Mustafa Kemal said in November 1918. "Military strength comes last.... Today it is not enough to have arms in hand in order to take one's place in the world as a human being."[9]

British Prime Minister Lloyd George viewed the nationalist uprising in Turkey as an inconvenience, an unforgivable chal- lenge to Allied authority that must be stamped out. It proved to be much more, however. From the ashes of World War I, a new world was rising up, a world that would see the crumbling of once-mighty empires, the creation of new borders and new nations. In many parts of the world—in Turkey; in Arabia; in Mesopotamia, Palestine, and Syria; and even in the "crown jewel" of the British Empire, India—the decisions made in the aftermath of World War I would echo.

The leaders who gathered to negotiate the terms of a peace treaty with Turkey—the treaty that would become the Treaty of Sèvres—believed that they were ensuring the collapse of the Ottoman Empire. They did not know that they were ensuring the collapse of their own empires as well.

When an artificial boundary line is drawn in a place other than where it had been, conflict frequently arises. Boundaries by their very nature imply a division, a separation between what belongs on one side and what belongs on the other. When boundaries are created artificially and are simply lines drawn on a map by outsiders with little knowledge of the people or the terrain that they are separating, conflict is inevitable.

2

The Rise
of an Empire

To the foreign observer, the modern Middle East seems to be a region marked by violence. Leaders and governments rise and fall quickly as the people struggle to determine how best their land should be ruled. There is a sense of uncertainty that marks Middle Eastern politics—an understanding that actions must be taken rapidly to avoid external and internal conflict and an awareness that borders are arbitrary and reflect separations that may or may not exist. It is a climate that gives rise to strong, frequently autocratic leaders determined to place a permanent stamp on their territory.

The violence and conflict that mark so much of life in the modern Middle East are not just the result of a gradual evolution of people and philosophies over time. They are instead a legacy of a point in time when the fate of the region was determined by actions taken thousands of miles away as a result of the thoughts, ideas, and prejudices of foreign leaders.

The modern Middle East, with its borders separating such lands as Iraq, Turkey, Syria, Saudi Arabia, and Israel, aptly illustrates how arbitrary boundaries can reshape a region. In fact, the very term "Middle East"—or "Near East," as the region was once called—serves as an imperfect label that implies a geographical generality viewed from a Western perspective.

The countries of the Middle East, however, now divided into small states and kingdoms, provide a stark contrast between the rich heritage of an ancient past and the results of weakened empires and Western meddling. The Treaty of Sèvres, intended as a means to exert greater Western control in the region, instead provided a reflection of the vast differences that divided "East" from "West" and of the dangers caused by a foreign power that placed arbitrary lines on a map and expected them to serve as effective borders.

HISTORY, INTERRUPTED

The history of the lands of the Middle East tells of advanced ancient civilizations whose achievements were truly remarkable. Fragments of these civilizations uncovered by archeological digs reveal glimpses of the culture and life that once flourished. It was in the Middle East that the Assyrians and the Sumerians built their empires, ruling over the region for 2,000 years before slipping into the sand. Ancient cuneiform inscriptions provide testimony of the development of some of the earliest forms of written language. Still later empires in Persia and Babylon sparked different achievements—the flourishing of poetry in Persia, the creation of the first code of laws in Babylon.

Rather than developing in a kind of isolation, this land was marked by invasion and conquest. Different portions, at different times, formed part of the Roman Empire, the Greek Empire, and even the Egyptian Empire. Different languages developed, spread, and then disappeared over time. Different cultures, in different parts of the Middle East, flourished and then vanished. Different systems of belief developed in the same way. Even in ancient times, there was no single belief system, no single language or culture that defined the area we now call the Middle East.

In the seventh and eighth centuries, conquerors from the Arabian Peninsula swept up into what was then part of the Roman Empire. They brought with them a new language—Arabic—and a new religion—Islam. Beginning as the language and religion of conquerors, these two entities would gradually spread throughout the region.

The Arabic word *Islam* can be translated as "surrender"—the believer is thought to surrender to God, and God alone—and *Muslim* is the believer or person who surrenders. For believers, and certainly for the Arabs who brought their religion into the lands that had once formed part of the Christian Roman Empire, Islam was not a revolutionary belief system. It was, instead, a continuation of the Jewish and Christian faiths that preceded it, a kind of final chapter contained in the revelations of the last and greatest of the prophets, Muhammad.[10] For Muslims, the teachings of Muhammad, inscribed in their holy book, the *Koran*, provided the final authority—a system of both belief and practice, of law and morality—over the lands they ruled.

Unlike many earlier religions and belief systems that had dominated in the Middle East, however, the period of Islamic rule in its earliest days was remarkable for its tolerance and diversity. Many Jews, Christians, and Zoroastrians lived in the Islamic territory. They were not forced to convert. They could accumulate great wealth. Their places of worship were not destroyed, although on occasion they were taken over and converted into mosques. They were allowed to practice their religion. In exchange for acknowledging the dominance of the Islamic state and paying a tax (which Muslims did not have to pay), they were promised security for their lives and property, protection against external enemies, freedom of worship, and independence in their own affairs. In this, the Muslims were markedly different from many of the rulers dominating other parts of the globe.

Although tolerance is not a word frequently used to define the modern Middle East, in ancient times tolerance was practiced. The greatest opportunities, of course, were reserved for free, male Muslims, but here again an important principle was imported with Islamic conquerors: the idea of equality among Muslims, regardless of where within the Islamic empire they resided. Unlike many other civilizations that placed great importance on inheritance and carved up the social order into various strata of rulers and noblemen to create elaborate systems of rank and class, the early Islamic states were noteworthy for their freedom of opportunity. For those male Muslims who were willing to work hard and for those who were talented, the Islamic state offered many chances to achieve wealth and power.

THE OTTOMANS

By the eleventh century, the empire that the Arabs had built based on Islamic ideals began to crumble. Internal fighting among different tribes and peoples, the rise of military leaders, and attacks from Europe and Africa all served to weaken and, ultimately, splinter the army. One of the most significant transformations came from the east, where the inhabitants of the steppes, called Turks, had gradually gained power. Known as particularly fierce and aggressive fighters, the Turks had been brought into Islamic territory as slaves, trained for military service rather than domestic service. They gradually made up more and more of the military forces, and as power within the Islamic kingdom shifted to the military, the Turks grew more powerful. They battled fiercely with the Crusaders who arrived in the region in 1096 and then later with the Mongols, led by Genghis Khan. The tilt of Islam, under Turkish leadership, began to shift to a more militant approach. Facing external and internal challenges, the Islamic religion under Turkish leadership became a more central part of political decision-making.

In the early part of the fourteenth century, a new invading force swept over the region. Led by the powerful leader known as Osman, the Ottoman forces (who took their name from their leader) rode west from central and northeast Asia, seizing the land over which they traveled. The Ottomans were Turkish speakers and followers of Islam, and they rapidly built a mighty empire, seizing portions of Europe and the Balkan Peninsula and defeating the Serbs, the Bulgurs, and the Macedonians.

In fact, the rise and fall of the Ottoman Empire was marked by treaties with Europe. Shortly after their conquest of portions of Europe, the Ottomans were approached by the Genoese (people from Genoa, Italy), who were at war with the Venetians. The Genoese asked the Ottomans for military help, promising financial aid in exchange. In 1352, a commercial treaty was signed between the two powers.

The Ottomans astutely combined the powerful forces of the military and Islamic beliefs into a single political system that supported their conquest and rule. The Ottomans instituted a new political hierarchy—a group of educated, professional religious leaders given specific powers over specific regions, all reporting to a supreme religious authority.[11]

In 1453, Ottoman forces successfully captured the city of Constantinople, a seizure of tremendous political and religious significance. The region had once been dominated by the Hittites, then the Persians, and still later by the armies of

Alexander the Great and the Romans. In A.D. 300, the Roman emperor Constantine had decided to build a new city on the site of the ancient city of Byzantium and called it Constantinople. From that glittering capital, an entire empire—the Byzantine Empire—had spread into Asia and the Balkan Peninsula.

The Ottomans recognized the strategic and political significance of capturing Constantinople and decided to make it their own capital, as the seaport on the seven hills. The sultan built a palace there, cementing the significance of the city's conquest and the symbolic union of the two portions of the Ottoman Empire: Europe and Asia. The city's name would eventually be changed to Istanbul. The Christian church Santa Sophia—the Church of Holy Wisdom, dating back to A.D. 537—would be transformed into the mosque Hagia Sophia. Christian symbols were removed from the interior, replaced by verses from the Koran or other Islamic texts. A crescent was added to the cathedral's dome, as were four minarets. The faithful would be called to prayer in Constantinople, and the city would once more reign over an empire, but the empire would be an Islamic one.

A SHIFT IN POWER

Successive generations of Ottoman rulers seized territory in Asia and Europe, twice advancing as far as Vienna before being forced to withdraw. It was, in fact, as a result of the second attempt by the Ottoman forces to push into southeastern Europe that a shift began in the relationship between European and Ottoman forces, marking a change in the balance of power.

In 1683, Turkish forces made an attempt to seize Vienna. It was the second Ottoman attempt on the city; more than a century earlier, Ottoman forces had advanced across southeastern Europe, gobbling up territory as they went before finally battling to a draw with Hapsburg (Habsburg) forces. The second attempt produced a very different result, however. For 60 days, Turkish forces camped outside Vienna before finally withdrawing in defeat. They fought fiercely during their long retreat, losing many battles and much territory as they withdrew.

It was a bitter loss for the Ottoman forces, and the peace treaty that they were forced to sign on January 26, 1699—the Peace Treaty of Carlowitz—marked a new era in relations between European and Ottoman forces. In earlier eras, any treaties that the Ottoman rulers had signed had been dictated on their terms, because they were the conquerors. The Treaty of Carlowitz was negotiated not between equals, however. With the Ottoman forces in the uncomfortable position of having lost many important battles, they had to agree to terms dictated by their enemies. The Ottoman leadership decided that they needed to adopt a new strategy: They turned to diplomacy, seeking to form alliances with Western European countries like England and Holland to offer a balance of power to the European countries located on Ottoman borders.[12] It would prove a fateful decision.

This changed diplomatic policy reflected a shift in economic policy as well. Even before the Peace Treaty of Carlowitz, in 1536 the Ottoman Empire had signed an agreement with France that was designed to encourage commercial exchange. The treaty, known as the Capitulation Agreement, allowed French merchants to trade freely within the Ottoman empire, to import and export their goods at low tariff rates, and to be exempt from Ottoman taxes. In addition, French merchants were made exempt from Ottoman (Islamic) law—instead, they were given extraterritorial privileges in which all legal matters would be referred to the French consul in Istanbul.

Soon, similar agreements were signed with other European countries. These agreements were all negotiated at a time when the Ottoman Empire was clearly superior militarily to the countries with which it was negotiating, but an increase in sophisticated European weaponry and tactics soon brought that time to an end. Gradually, the balance of power began to shift away from the Ottoman Empire and toward the European nations. The results proved devastating to the Ottoman economy.

European goods flooded into the Ottoman Empire. By the nineteenth century, European merchants dominated the Ottoman economy; they were able to operate freely, enjoying advantages that local merchants did not have. The European merchants were exempt from local taxes. They could conduct their business with minimal interference from the government, and much less expensively than the empire's subjects could. Any legal matters were referred to the European merchant's own consul, making the consuls extraordinarily powerful and frequently corrupt and resulting in the dropping of many criminal cases by the respective consuls. No foreigner could be seized or arrested by Ottoman police unless a representative from his consul was present.

Soon, Ottoman merchants who wanted to compete needed to become foreigners in their own country. *Berats*—documents that could be purchased from a consulate or an embassy to entitle the owner to the same rights as a national of that country—were freely sold, and a black market sprung up in passports and citizenship papers.

As European goods flooded their marketplaces, as Europeans increasingly controlled their own economy, and as foreigners began to enjoy a better standard of living than the citizens of the Ottoman Empire, the climate grew ripe for revolt.

YOUNG TURKS

By the early part of the twentieth century, the Ottoman Empire had grown increasingly corrupt. The corruption was clearest in regard to the sultan—the ruler of the empire—and his family. One by one, sultans were murdered or forced into exile, and family members seized the throne from each other in a continuous quest for power. A huge gap had arisen between the wealthiest members of society—the royal family, wealthy landowners, and religious and military leaders—and the poorest—peasants, farmers, and some craftsmen. Operating in the middle, increasingly dominating the exchange of goods and services, were Westerners. With them they brought Western influences and more modern European ideas. The wealthiest members of the empire—and the foreign merchants—paid no taxes to support the lavish lifestyle of the sultan and his family.

The sultan Abdul Hamid ruled over an Ottoman Empire weakened by revolts, corruption, and loss of territory. In 1909, Abdul Hamid was deposed and his younger brother, Mehmed V, was proclaimed the new sultan.

Although the opportunities for corruption in the Ottoman Empire had increased as the nineteenth century gave way to the twentieth, the actual size of the empire had decreased. Important territories had been lost to Greece, and Great Britain was occupying Egypt.

The sultan, Abdul Hamid, sensed that his power was slipping away. Rumors of revolution, once murmured quietly in the farthest outposts of the empire, were now being discussed in the streets of the capital city. Hamid was determined to tighten his grip on the empire. He suspended the constitution, disbanded parliament, and enlisted the help of secret police to spy on his people. The punishment for those who disagreed with his policies was severe.

The Ottoman Empire still dominated a sizable territory, however. Although the sultan's control and the reach of his secret police were strong in the capital, they were much weaker in the farther reaches of the empire. The borders that outlined the Ottoman Empire were more arbitrary in many of the territories far from Istanbul, where discontent spread and loyalties to tribe or family mattered more than loyalty to the sultan.

In the port town of Salonica (in a region now forming part of Greece), the powerful Ottoman third army had its headquarters. Many in the military viewed the sultan's actions with alarm. They were, in a sense, quite conservative in their views. They did not dream of revolution in the traditional sense—of establishing a completely new system of government. Instead, they believed that the trouble lay with the sultan himself; they felt that his corrupt rule was weakening the empire. They wanted to see the empire restored to its former glory—with a strong military as one of its marks of achievement.

Abdul Hamid knew that members of the military were plotting against him. He was determined to keep them weak by refusing to provide them with decent equipment and weaponry and frequently by not paying their salaries.

Of course, these decisions encouraged more members of the military to join with those plotting reform. The protests were not exclusive to the military. Exiles living in Europe, discouraged civil servants and merchants, and even students had formed a secret protest society in the late 1800s, known as the Committee of Union and Progress (C.U.P.). As the protests spread to the military, officers (many of them educated in

European-style military academies) had formed their own groups linked to the C.U.P.

The clues to the aims of this protest movement lay in its members. These were not oppressed members of the working class such as farmers, peasants, and the poor. Instead, the C.U.P. was led by young officers in the army, men who had no interest in eliminating the class system but instead wanted the opportunity that previous generations had enjoyed—to serve in one of the most powerful militaries in the world. They wanted to restore the empire to its former glory.

By the summer of 1908, a group of officers from the third army had staged a revolt. They demanded that the sultan restore the constitution, threatening to march on Istanbul with an army of 100,000 men and to restore it themselves (naming the sultan's heir as the new sultan) if he did not immediately respond. For two days, Abdul Hamid attempted to find a way out before reluctantly agreeing to their demands. The constitution was restored, and elections for a new parliament were held in the fall of 1908.

For a brief period, peace was restored. The sultan was once more popular; the army that had staged the revolt was cheered in the streets. The forces unleashed by the leaders of the C.U.P. had staggering consequences, however. The "Young Turks," as they were called, had plenty of patriotism but little political experience. They spoke the phrases that they had learned while studying in Europe or in European-style military academies, phrases like "Liberty, Equality, Fraternity, Justice." They viewed these as phrases that described the glory days of the Ottoman Empire; they were nostalgic for a time when the empire had dominated whatever it sought to conquer. More important, however, they sought to recreate an empire in which Turks, not Europeans or a corrupt elite, dominated.

The ideals of the phrase "Liberty, Equality, Fraternity, Justice" that appeared on banners proudly unfurled by the C.U.P. meant very different things in the more remote parts of the empire. The revolution, which had been begun by the young military officers to pull the empire together, instead caused more pieces to split off. As the Young Turks spoke of freedom and equality and recalled with nostalgia a distant past, other revolutionaries within the empire dreamed of independence and a future marked by new borders.

Within three months, the Ottoman-held territory of Bulgaria declared its independence. Austria seized the Ottoman provinces of Bosnia and Herzegovina. Crete voted to unite with Greece. Newspapers, freed from restrictions and censorship by the new laws, quickly published criticism of the leaders, complaints against governmental corruption, and, perhaps most significant, information about governmental policies—and their failures.

Previous generations had viewed with alarm the rapid Westernization of the Ottoman Empire. The sultan had decided to crack down on challenges to his authority, and the C.U.P. was determined to limit the powers of a corrupt monarchy. Yet another change quickly swept over the empire. A counterrevolution against the new government was sparked by a group of theological students and ordinary soldiers who felt that the empire needed to return to traditional Islamic law, known as *sharia*. Troops were sent to Istanbul in April 1909 to protect the capital and the government. On the night of April 12, however, the troops mutinied and were joined by teachers and students from religious schools in the city. They marched on the parliament building, forcing the government officials there to run for their lives. Members of the C.U.P. were forced into hiding. Those who were found were executed. Within 24 hours, Abdul Hamid agreed to the revolutionaries' demands to appoint a new head of government to follow sharia.

The C.U.P. quickly reorganized in Salonica, the distant city in which the military had first organized its revolt. An armed force marched to Istanbul, camping outside the city while a fleet of ships surrounded it by water. Istanbul was quickly seized; the leaders of the counterrevolution were captured and, in many cases, hanged.

The C.U.P. suspected the sultan of supporting the counterrevolutionaries. At the least, he had agreed to their demands too quickly. A special session of parliament was convened, and a vote was quickly taken: The sultan was to be deposed. Permission was also obtained from a religious leader, Sheikh al-Islam, who agreed to the deposition, thus satisfying both the religious and the political authorities. A group of officers went to the palace to deliver the news. The sultan was then allowed to gather a few of his possessions and board a train for Salonica.

The sultan's younger brother, Mehmed V, was proclaimed the new sultan. He made it clear that he would not pose any significant challenge to the new political forces rushing through Istanbul. He had spent a lifetime surrounded by his brother's spies, his servants, and the ladies of his harem; he had not read a newspaper in 20 years.[13]

HOPES OF REFORM

The new regime that ruled over the Ottoman Empire was intent on creating reforms that would restore the empire's pride, its vitality, and its economic success. The task was enormous. They were determined to review nearly every aspect of society, replacing those portions that had become corrupt or outdated with new systems. They focused on taxes, the status of women, and the press. Above all, they focused on creating a new national identity—on the idea of Ottomanism as a source of national pride. Divisions sparked by the revolutionary ideals grew more apparent as the empire continued to splinter. Differences between Muslims and other religious groups in the empire continued to widen. The borders that marked the limits of the Ottoman Empire were fading. The loss of Bulgaria, Bosnia and Herzegovina, and Crete made it clear that in certain parts of the empire, regional identity was stronger than a national identity.

The empire that the Young Turks struggled to bring together under a single, common identity was simply too vast and too different. It contained numerous religious groups, numerous languages, and numerous ethnic identities. The empire that had stretched from Europe to Asia was now stretched too thin. Its

This photo shows Archduke of Austria Franz Ferdinand and his wife Sophie, just moments before they were assassinated in 1914 in Sarajevo. Austria's subsequent invasion of Serbia set off the chain of events that led to World War I.

citizens no longer viewed themselves as such. Borders that had once seemed clear and definite now felt artificial and arbitrary.

By 1912, the empire had lost Libya to Italian forces. It had lost Macedonia. Serbia had won its autonomy. Greek forces threatened on the border. Arab nationalist groups had formed in Beirut, Damascus, and Baghdad. Following a series of wars in the Balkans, nearly all Ottoman territory in Europe had been lost.

The Young Turks took dramatic steps to ensure that no further territory would be lost. They centralized all governmental operations and exercised much firmer control, with power resting principally in the hands of three Young Turks: Enver Bey, Talat Bey, and Jemal Pasha. Under their leadership, a kind of three-way dictatorship oversaw all aspects of life in the empire. Those who disagreed with the leaders were punished or killed. The press was once more censored.

To deal with the embarrassing defeats in the Balkan Wars, the Young Turks also decided to reform the military. Admiring the accomplishments of the German armed forces, the Young Turks arranged for German experts to come into the empire to help reform the military. German instructors soon headed up the military academies, and German officers were added to army units.

This relationship between the military and Germany dramatically affected the fate of the Ottoman Empire. On June 28, 1914, the Austrian Archduke Ferdinand was assassinated in Sarajevo, setting in motion a chain of events that would lead the world to war. Austria invaded Serbia, triggering the activation of a series of alliances that been designed previously among the various powers in Europe. Soon, Great Britain, France, and Russia had aligned against Germany and Austria-Hungary.

At first, the Ottoman Empire seemed likely to pursue a policy of neutrality, but ultimately those within the government who were aligned with Germany helped swing the empire into a position of support for the Central Powers. They viewed it as an opportunity to strike out against Russia, which had long threatened Ottoman territories, and to once more seize British-held Egypt. On August 2, 1914, Jemal Pasha, Talat Bey, and Enver Bey signed an alliance with Germany, which was really an alliance against Russia.

This alliance remained secret for several weeks as members of the Ottoman Empire met with representatives from the Allies—Russia, England, and France—about the possibility of joining them. The Allies felt that the Ottomans' demands—including an end to the hated capitulations—were too high. They believed that the Ottoman Empire possessed little in the way of military strength and that its defeat could easily be accomplished. Russia was eager to seize Istanbul and gain control of the Turkish Straits. The British were eager to protect their routes to India. France was interested in Syrian territory. The Allied powers decided to refuse the Ottoman request for an alliance and instead allow it to join forces with Germany. When the war was over, the empire could then easily be divided among them, with new borders marking the territories they planned to control.

On October 29, 1914, Ottoman ships sailed up the Bosporus into the Black Sea, attacking several Russian ports and destroying Russian ships. The Ottoman Empire was once more at war, but this war would be its last.

3

The Wages
of War

In the early years of the conflict that became known as World War I, it was clear that the Allied nations had underestimated the strength and skills of the Ottoman army. The military had been the focus of much of the government's efforts following the disastrous Balkan Wars, and the rigorous training and new tactics taught by German officers had transformed the Ottoman forces into a much more effective fighting machine.

The vastness of the Ottoman Empire posed a special challenge to the military charged with defending it. There were multiple points of entry, presenting the Allies with numerous potential places for attack. Along the eastern borders of Anatolia and the region of the Caucasus, Ottoman forces clashed with Russian troops. The fighting was fierce, and the conflict produced an even more horrific legacy, one that remains one of the most brutal moments in the history of the Ottoman Empire.

The eastern border region of Anatolia was the home to a large Armenian population. Many of them remained loyal to the sultan and the Ottoman government, but nationalist leaders within the population saw the war and the Russian incursions as an opportunity to strike out against the Ottoman regime in the hope of creating an independent Armenia. They allied themselves with the Russians; in some areas of Anatolia, armed bands of Armenian guerrillas seized control of towns and villages, whereas others joined the Russian forces.

The Ottoman government took a severe step to stamp out this rebellion. In early 1915, it issued an order to deport and relocate the Armenian population of Anatolia. Certain Armenians— specifically railway workers, members of the armed forces, Catholics, and Protestants—were exempt from deportation, but the vast majority of Armenian men, women, and children were not. Hundreds of thousands were forced from their homes and sent on a forced march south, toward the Syrian Desert. The straggling lines of Armenians soon dwindled as countless numbers fell victim to hunger, disease, exhaustion, and exposure. Others were killed before they left Anatolia, still more along the way. It is not known exactly how many Armenians died as a

In 1915, these Armenian soldiers from the Caucasus region joined forces with Russia in its war against the Ottoman Empire. While many Armenians remained loyal to the Ottoman government, others saw an opportunity to create an independent state of Armenia. Ottoman retaliation forced many Armenians, complicit or not, from their homes and claimed the lives of approximately one million people.

result of this death march, but the estimates often fall close to one million people.

Yet another group within the Ottoman Empire, the Arabs, viewed the war as an opportunity to strike out for their independence. The Arabs also chose to ally themselves with an Allied power—in this case, the British. They had a geographic advantage that aided their efforts. Unlike the Armenians, who lived within Turkey's eastern territory and were surrounded by a large Muslim population, the Arabs chose to begin their independence movement in the Hijaz region of Arabia. Far from Istanbul and far from Turkey, this region was governed not by a C.U.P. leader but instead by Sharif Hussain, an Arab hereditary ruler, and was a region that was both Arab and Muslim. In the Hijaz,

Sharif Hussain governed the two holiest cities in all of the Muslim faith—Mecca and Medina.

A revolt sparked in Islam's holiest territory, in which the Ottoman sultan was being cast aside by the ruler of Mecca and Medina, certainly presented an attractive tool to the empire that governed more Muslims than any other—the British Empire. It is not surprising that the British agreed to support (and in fact helped nurture) the group of Bedouin warriors who led the Arab revolt. The Arabian Peninsula was within easy access of British forces in Egypt. They were happy to encourage the Arabs in their rebellion, but what was promised in exchange created intense disputes in the postwar years.

There is little doubt that Sharif Hussain was promised an independent Hijaz region. He was in fact told that he would be made "king of the Arabs." Precisely where this kingdom would begin and end was never formally determined, its borders never marked clearly on a map. Hussain envisioned himself ruler of a vast Islamic empire stretching north into Palestine and south to the Persian Gulf and encompassing Syria and Mesopotamia (modern-day Iraq). The British were meeting with other Arab leaders as well, however, and had little intention of creating a vast Islamic empire that could threaten their "crown jewel," India. The location of the borders that would denote Sharif Hussain's "Arab kingdom" was left deliberately vague.

VICTORY AND DEFEAT

Although the Ottoman armies were fighting both internal and external forces, they fought successfully in the early years of the war. In early 1915, a combined Anglo-French force launched an attack on the Gallipoli Peninsula, threatening the very heart of the Ottoman Empire. The Ottoman forces, led by a young officer named Mustafa Kemal and aided by German officers, fought back fiercely, repelling numerous attempts by Allied forces to seize Gallipoli. For several months, the British and French forces fought on, suffering tremendous casualties. Although ultimately joined by Italian reinforcements, they still were unable to seize

Troops land at Anzac Cove in the Dardanelles during the battle between the Allied and Ottoman forces on the Gallipoli Peninsula. Fierce fighting on the Ottoman side, led by Mustafa Kemal and aided by German officers, led the Allied forces to withdraw in 1916.

Gallipoli. Finally, in January 1916, the Allied forces were forced to withdraw.

In the east, Ottoman forces had attempted to push into Russia and seize additional territory. The effort failed, and the remains of the Ottoman army retreated. By 1917, a revolution had swept through Russia, and the Russian military soon pulled back, allowing Ottoman forces to advance once more and to take back much of the territory that they had lost.

The Ottoman government also focused on Egypt during the early years of the war, attempting to push British forces out and take back the territory. On December 18, 1914, Great Britain formally declared that it was establishing a protectorate in Egypt, appointing a new sultan and fortifying its base along the Suez Canal, which became a target for later attacks. Ottoman forces, under the command of Jemal Pasha, launched a surprise attack in February 1915 and for the rest of the year periodically attacked at points along the canal. These raids accomplished little. A final massive assault began in mid-1916, but it never succeeded in recapturing the canal—or Egypt—from British forces.

As the war progressed in the regions of Syria, Egypt, and Palestine, the Ottoman forces were crippled by poor transportation systems and by sabotage of their supplies. The Arab revolt added to the challenge as raiding bands of Arabs launched guerrilla attacks on railways, bridges, and supply caravans. British forces were able to use their base in Egypt as a launching point for the region, seizing territory in Palestine, Syria, and Iraq.

By early 1917, British forces had occupied Gaza in Palestine and Baghdad in Mesopotamia (Iraq). Later in the year, they captured Jerusalem. In 1918, they seized Damascus in Syria. Still worse for the Ottoman forces, their German allies were no longer able to provide supplies or military assistance. Germany had suffered its own staggering losses in the war's Western Front in the summer of 1918 and was clearly facing defeat.

On October 29, 1918, a delegation from the Ottoman Empire boarded the British warship H.M.S. *Agamemnon,* based off the coast of Mudros on the island of Lemnos, where they met with the commander of the British Mediterranean fleet. Within 24 hours, an armistice had been signed, and the war in the Middle East was over. Less than two weeks later, Germany also signed an armistice. The Ottoman Empire had not agreed to a complete surrender, but the terms of the armistice did dictate that Ottoman forces would be demobilized and Allied forces would be given control of the Turkish Straits.

One significant point paved the way for the Treaty of Sèvres, the crisscrossing borders that would define the Middle East, and the conflict that would follow. Article VII of the armistice agreement stated, "The Allies have the right to occupy any strategic points in the event of any situation arising which threatens the security of the Allies."[14] This clause was a kind of blank check, permitting occupation of any portion of the Ottoman Empire for any reason deemed necessary.

Once victory was assured, the Allies could turn their attention to dividing up the remnants of the Ottoman Empire. It was a process that they had begun several years earlier.

CARVING UP THE EMPIRE

Long before World War I had ended, the Allied powers had looked ahead to the rich promise of new territory in the Ottoman Empire and had determined which pieces they most wanted to control. Although the British were meeting with Arab leaders and making promises of independent kingdoms, and the Russians were encouraging an Armenian independence movement, it is perhaps not surprising that none of these powers was operating altruistically, focusing on the needs of the citizens of the Ottoman Empire. In fact, they each had strategic interests in the region, interests that would benefit from additional territory and greater control. The borders that they intended to assign would be placed arbitrarily, to mark the beginning and end of Allied interests in the region.

Therefore, long before the war's end, the Allied powers had signed a series of agreements among themselves to determine how they would oversee the Ottoman territories and which Allied power would be placed in control of which portion of the empire. It was almost as if they were "reserving in advance" the future territory that they wanted after the war in the hope of resolving any potential postwar disputes before they arose.[15] These "advance bookings" reflect how arbitrary the borders were, as territories were divided long before conflict in the region had ended and well before the impact of the war on the former citizens of the Ottoman Empire could be studied or understood.

The first of these arbitrary border agreements was signed in March 1915. Known as the Constantinople Agreement, it gave Russia the right to annex Istanbul and the Turkish Straits. This agreement was never implemented; when the Russian Revolution occurred in November 1917, all previous treaties signed by the tsar were voided.

Next came the Sykes-Picot Agreement, secretly completed in

May 1916 by Great Britain and France. This gave France control of the Syrian coast and portions of southern Lebanon and Anatolia as well as the right to oversee most of Syria's interior region. Great Britain was given the right to direct control of southern Mesopotamia (Iraq) as well as a zone of exclusive influence in most of the region's northern and central territory, stretching up to Gaza. Palestine was to be governed by an international tribunal. The Arab territory promised to Sharif Hussain was, in the Sykes-Picot Agreement, instead divided up by arbitrary borders into a cluster of states placed under either French or British control.

THE SYKES-PICOT AGREEMENT

The Sykes-Picot Agreement was a secret understanding between representatives of Great Britain (Sir Mark Sykes) and France (François Georges Picot), concluded in May 1916 as World War I was being fought. The agreement proved to be one of the most controversial treaties of the wartime era, reneging on earlier promises that Great Britain had made (to the Arab leader Sharif Hussain, for one) and plotting a course for Great Britain and France to dismember the Ottoman Empire.

In it, Sykes and Picot mapped out the divisions of Syria, Iraq, Lebanon, and Palestine. The Ottoman Empire was essentially divided into French- and British-administered areas. The map marked the Middle East with bright blues and reds, the blue areas showing where France would exercise direct or indirect administration and the red marking British territory. A much smaller brown area marked a zone of international administration.

The agreement granted France a zone of "direct control" along the Syrian coast from southern Lebanon into Anatolia, as well as exclusive "indirect control" in the interior of Syria. Great Britain was granted the right to "direct control" over southern Mesopotamia (Iraq) and indirect control over a vast area stretching from Gaza to Kirkuk.

The Sykes-Picot agreement also promised the creation of an independent Arab state or confederation of states, placing it under indirect control of both the British and the French. The area of Palestine was designated to fall within international administration.

The question of Palestine's fate arose in yet another controversial agreement. Palestine was strategically important to British efforts to link their empires in Africa and Asia. With Great Britain in control of both Mesopotamia and Palestine, the British Empire would possess a land road from Egypt to India, adding to British-controlled territories in Persia (modern Iran). The goal of some British leaders was to add territory that would create a chain of dominions from the Atlantic to the Pacific.

In November 1917, a letter from British Foreign Secretary Arthur Balfour to a prominent British Zionist (who supported the idea of the creation of a Jewish state), known as the Balfour Declaration, formally stated that the British government would support the creation of a Jewish state in Palestine. The letter said, in part,

> His Majesty's Government view with favour the establishment in Palestine of a national home for the Jewish people, and will use their best endeavours to facilitate the achievement of this object, it being clearly understood that nothing shall be done which may prejudice the civil and religious rights of existing non-Jewish communities in Palestine, or the rights and political status enjoyed by Jews in any other country.[16]

Long before the Ottoman Empire had signed an armistice, its lands had been divided up by its enemies. Through agreements, treaties, and letters, the fate of the Middle East had been decided by men who, in many cases, had never been there. Borders and boundaries—many overlapping and contradictory—had been sketched out by men who did not understand what they were dividing.

A MEETING IN PARIS

In January 1919, a conference was organized in Paris to help resolve some of the conflicts created by previous agreements and to ensure that there would never again be a war like the one that the world had so recently experienced. Representatives from 27 nations arrived to create formal agreements that would resolve postwar disputes and determine the fate of the defeated nations.

The focus at first was on Germany and Austria-Hungary, and as 1919 unfolded four different treaties between the Allied powers and Germany, Bulgaria, and Hungary were signed. Resolving the Middle East question was not so speedily accomplished, having been made more challenging by the numerous agreements that had preceded the Paris Peace Conference. The conference had as its governing body the Supreme Council, which

THE FOURTEEN POINTS

On January 8, 1918, President Woodrow Wilson delivered a speech before the U.S. Congress that introduced the idea of a League of Nations—an organization that was designed to provide political independence for large and small nations. The speech, which became known as the "Fourteen Points," was intended to help end World War I and promote peace, an effort Wilson continued at the Paris Peace Conference in 1919. The charter for Wilson's planned League of Nations became part of the Treaty of Versailles.

These 14 points included a demand for open diplomacy that avoided private treaties and agreements; free navigation of all seas; equal trade among all nations; a reduction in weapons so that nations would retain only those necessary for domestic security; and the formation of a "general association of nations." Point V called for "a free, open-minded and absolutely impartial adjustment of all claims, based upon a strict observance of the principle that in determining all such questions of sovereignty the interests of the populations concerned must have equal weight with the equitable claims of the government whose title is to be determined."

The Fourteen Points were also specific on the question of the Ottoman Empire. Point XII noted that the Turkish portion "should be assured a secure sovereignty, but the other nationalities which are now under Turkish rule should be assured an undoubted security of life and an absolutely unmolested opportunity of autonomous development."

Wilson received the 1919 Nobel Peace Prize for his efforts, but he failed to win congressional support for U.S. entry into the League or approval of the treaty, a key (Wilson believed) to ensuring world peace.

determined the meeting's agenda and had the final vote on any and all decisions. Its members were Great Britain, France, Italy, the United States, and Japan. The majority of all decisions affecting the Middle East was made by Great Britain and France. Italy did give suggestions and recommendations, but some were followed and others were ignored. Representatives from the United States had little impact on the conference's outcome.

The goal of Great Britain in the Middle East was clear: to add to the security of the empire by expanding it. British officials focused on balancing any influence gained by their former allies, the French, by ensuring parity or, wherever possible, greater amounts of gained territory. Great Britain was determined to protect its interests in India by adding to land routes there, and it focused on protecting its sea route through the Suez Canal to its territory in Egypt. Its oil fields in Iran and Iraq were growing increasingly important and also required protection.

France, heavily battered by the war, was concerned more with containing Germany than adding to its territory in the Middle East. At the Paris Peace Conference, French representatives focused on acquiring additional land on the border with Germany (in the regions of Alsace-Lorraine and Saar) and obtaining reparations from Germany. Initially hoping to gain control of Syria, Palestine, and northern Iraq, the French finally and reluctantly agreed to compromise in order to ensure British support of their claims against Germany. France agreed to take control of the northern portion of Syria (the area that today makes up Syria and Lebanon), and Great Britain retained control of the region's oil fields.

What of the Ottoman representatives to the Peace Conference? A delegation had, in fact, been sent, headed by an unelected representative of the sultan named Damat Ferit Paşa. Paşa's strategy was to concede as much as possible in order to appease the Allied powers while retaining as much territory as he could and doing his best to overthrow the C.U.P. government. Paşa agreed with any charges made by the Allies against the Ottoman Empire, blaming each and every charge—true or false—on the C.U.P.

government. Because that government was no longer in power, Paşa argued, there was no need for excessively harsh recriminations against the Ottoman Empire. Paşa proposed that the Ottoman Empire should retain control of the Mosul region of Mesopotamia (what we know today as northern Iraq) as well as Anatolia. Paşa proposed that the sultan appoint new governors to rule over the provinces in Arabia, granting them limited autonomy. Furthermore, he proposed that any questions regarding the border with the Armenians should be negotiated by the Ottoman government. Finally, he argued that there was no need for any European nation to establish mandates in any portion of the Middle East.

Paşa's bluster—his proposals hardly reflected the Ottoman Empire's status as a defeated and humbled nation—sparked astonishment at first and then outright laughter. The British were not laughing, however; they were furious.

The official response of the Allied powers to Paşa's proposals was delivered by Great Britain in words that did not describe the scorn for the Ottoman Empire felt by Prime Minister David Lloyd George and his representatives:

> ... there is no case to be found, either in Europe or Asia or Africa, in which the establishment of Ottoman rule in any country has not been followed by the diminution of its material prosperity, and a fall in its level of culture; nor is there any case to be found in which the withdrawal of Ottoman rule has not been followed by a growth in material prosperity and a rise in the level of culture. Neither among the Christians of Europe, nor among the Moslems of Syria, Arabia and Africa has the Ottoman Turk done other than destroy what he has conquered; never has he shown himself able to develop in peace what he has won by war.[17]

UNREST AND UNCERTAINTY

The various representatives at the Paris Peace Conference were unable to reach a consensus about the fate of the Middle East, and so the signing of a peace treaty between the Allied powers and the Ottoman Empire was postponed. Armies of the Allied powers continued to occupy significant portions of the Middle East. The people of the region, frustrated by the postponement of the treaty and by the presence of foreign troops in their lands, grew increasingly vocal in their demands for the right to govern themselves. Different political forces jockeyed for position in the region. Disputes arose between different Arab leaders about who would be given the right to serve as "king of Arabia" and about where that kingdom would begin and end. Sharif Hussein believed that his territory would include Palestine—a clear contradiction of the promise made in the Balfour Declaration. His son Faysal had helped lead the Arab revolt against the Ottoman armies and now held control of territory in the Hijaz region of Arabia as well as Syria—a conflict with France's plans to govern Syria.

Even the Allied armies maintaining control over these disputed territories were restless. The British forces who now policed territory from Palestine to Egypt, from Mosul to the Persian Gulf, were young volunteers who had enlisted to fight in the war. Now that the war was over, they wanted to go home.

U.S. President Wilson had hoped to help the Middle East achieve self-rule, as outlined in his Fourteen Points, which were drawn up to serve as a framework for his planned League of Nations. Wilson was seriously ill in 1919, however, and could not influence the decision-making process as he had hoped. Political sentiment in America was opposed to any mandates in the Middle East.

Great Britain and France were determined to take control of the situation and to resolve the question of the Middle East once and for all. Both were under pressure to reduce their military presence in the region, and the amount of violence was growing. There were anti-Jewish riots in Palestine. Faysal had seized Syria and had himself appointed king. His brother, Sharif Hussain's oldest son, Abdullah, was attempting to have himself named king of Iraq.

In April 1920, the representatives of the Allied powers again gathered to attempt to resolve the situation in the Middle East. They met at the Italian resort town of San Remo, on the Riviera, where they mapped out their plans for the mandates, the policies toward Turks and Arabs, and control of the region's oil. Their decisions would form the framework of a new peace agreement, one that would be known as the Treaty of Sèvres.

4

A Separate
Peace

When peace negotiations between the Allied powers and the Ottoman Empire finally began, British Prime Minister Lloyd George had predicted that it would take about a week for an agreement to be reached.[18] In fact, beginning with the informal discussions between France's premier Georges Clemenceau and Great Britain's Lloyd George immediately after the armistice was signed, it took nearly a year and a half for any kind of substantive agreement to be reached and another four months for the agreement to be finalized and a treaty to be signed.

The issues confronting the Allied powers and the Ottoman Empire were complex, made more complicated by the ambitions of nations like Great Britain and France, who wished to seize or retain territory in the Middle East. Meetings like the first Conference of London (in February 1920) exposed both the prejudices and the ambitions of the Allied powers when it came to the Ottoman Empire.

As the Allied powers met again and again, engaging in a constant round of peace conferences and discussions, the situation in the Middle East evolved, changing the dynamic of the meetings and moving the discussions beyond their focus on a postwar Ottoman Empire. Lloyd George was under increasing pressure to reduce the size of the British military presence overseas. Unrest swept over the Ottoman territory as the lack of a decisive treaty demonstrated an absence of a strong overriding authority. The Ottoman sultan Mehmed VI, who had taken the throne in June 1918, was intent on keeping the throne and did not hesitate to take the steps he deemed necessary to preserve his reign—that is, to appease the British authorities in Istanbul. As rumors of what the Allies had in mind for the Ottoman lands began to spread, certain politicians in Istanbul began to speak out against the likely Allied claims and actions. These politicians were quickly suppressed; the sultan abolished parliament, appointing his brother-in-law to serve as his second-in-command. Soon a split had been created between those who supported the sultan and those who were actively working to overthrow him, and both of these groups attempted to work

The Ottoman sultan Mehmed VI took the Turkish throne in June 1918 and held it until nationalists established a Turkish republic in 1922.

through the Allied powers to influence the outcome of their conferences and the future plans for the empire.

Beyond the borders of Istanbul (where British troops patrolled the harbor), chaos reigned. No clear authority was in charge; various groups began to riot or to seize property and land. Fuel was scarce; the fate of the Ottoman Empire seemed as dim and bleak as the cold, dark city of Istanbul.

THE TREATY OF SÈVRES

Finally, in April 1920, the Allied powers meeting in San Remo reached basic agreements on how best to divide up the Middle East. These agreements were drafted into written form and presented to the Ottoman sultan. On August 10, 1920, in the Parisian suburb of Sèvres, the peace treaty between the former Allied powers and the representatives of the Ottoman government was finally signed.

Although the main points of the treaty were principally the handiwork of Great Britain and France, the document officially noted that the "Principal Allied Powers" included Great Britain, France, Italy, and Japan, joined by the so-called "Allied Powers"—Armenia, Belgium, Greece, the Hijaz (part of modern Saudi Arabia), Poland, Portugal, Romania, Czechoslovakia, and what was described as "the Serb-Croat-Slovene State," a region that later became Yugoslavia. The treaty was designed to represent this formidable group of nations on the one hand and Turkey on the other.

The Treaty of Sèvres contains in its very opening the inspiring phrase,

> Whereas the Allied Powers are equally desirous that the war in which certain among them were successively involved, directly or indirectly, against Turkey, and which originated in the declaration of war against Serbia on July 28, 1914, by the former Imperial and Royal Austro-Hungarian Government, and in the hostilities opened by Turkey against the Allied Powers on October 29, 1914, and conducted by Germany in alliance with Turkey, should be replaced by a firm, just and durable Peace.

The peace planned by the Allied powers and spelled out in detail in the treaty's terms was far from just, however. All the Arabic-speaking parts of the Ottoman Empire—Syria, Palestine, Mesopotamia (Iraq), and the Hijaz (in Arabia)—were to be taken by and divided between Great Britain and France. Great Britain would retain Mesopotamia and Palestine; Arabia would

gain its independence but would be governed by monarchs chosen by Great Britain who were friendly to its interests. Egypt and
the lands along the Persian Gulf would remain British-held territory. Syria, including the region we now know as Lebanon,
would be given to France. Greece was to be given most of the
Aegean Islands and eastern Thrace (in the European section of
Turkey). Greece would also be given the task of administering
western Anatolia, including its major city, Smyrna, for five years.
After five years, a vote was to be held, and the citizens could then
decide whether they wished to become part of Greece. In eastern
Anatolia, Armenia was given its independence, and Kurdistan
was given autonomy. The Dardanelles were placed under international control.

The harsh terms spelled out the ways in which the Ottoman
Empire would be stripped not only of its territory but also of its
very independence. The Ottoman finances were to be placed
under the joint control of Great Britain, France, and Italy.
Foreigners would oversee essentially all aspects of the region's
economic life. Lloyd George had reluctantly agreed, after much
argument, to allow Istanbul to remain in the hands of the
Ottoman sultan, and the city and the small portion of Turkish-
speaking Anatolia left were all that remained for the Ottoman
ruler to govern.

Printing the Treaty of Sèvres in its entirety would require a
much longer book. It is helpful to examine certain of its clauses,
however, to understand better the points of conflict its arbitrary
borders sparked in the Middle East. The artificial boundaries
called for in the Treaty of Sèvres divided terrain and people that
had been united for centuries. Certain groups were deemed wor-
thy of a homeland of their own; others were separated from the
very lands that were critical to their way of life.

KURDISTAN

In its third section, the Treaty of Sèvres addressed the issue of
an autonomous region for the Kurdish peoples, to be known as
Kurdistan. Article 62 noted,

A Commission sitting at Constantinople and composed of three members appointed by the British, French and Italian Governments respectively shall draft within six months from the coming into force of the present Treaty a scheme of local autonomy for the predominantly Kurdish areas lying east of the Euphrates, south of the southern boundary of Armenia as it may be hereafter determined, and north of the frontier of Turkey with Syria and Mesopotamia.

In Article 64, the clear promise of autonomy was spelled out:

If within one year from the coming into force of the present Treaty the Kurdish peoples within the areas defined in Article 62 shall address themselves to the Council of the League of Nations in such a manner as to show that a majority of the population of these areas desires independence from Turkey, and if the Council then considers that these peoples are capable of such independence and recommends that it should be granted to them, Turkey hereby agrees to execute such a recommendation, and to renounce all rights and title over these areas.

The treaty specifically promised the Kurds a homeland, but what they were being offered was far less than they had hoped for. Missing from the region specified by Article 62 was much of the traditional Kurdish land—land that lay to the west of the Euphrates River, land that according to the terms of the treaty had been granted to France. The oil-rich region of Mosul had also been separated from the proposed boundaries of "Kurdistan." The people of Mosul were to be offered the opportunity to vote on whether they wished to become part of Kurdistan only after it had become an independent state and only if the Allied powers first determined that the people were capable of making that decision.

Missing from Kurdistan were the Kurds' most fertile regions, the grazing grounds and the valuable stretches of land that were in Persia (modern-day Iran). The Kurds were being offered the promise of their own land, but it was a much poorer and smaller land than the territory that had traditionally been Kurdish. That had instead been portioned off among the Allies, who clustered around the Kurdish borders.

ARMENIA

The Armenians, whose brutal massacre during the war had roused public anger and dismay in Europe, received the promise, in Article 88, of recognition as a "free and independent State." Article 89 further specified that the border that would be set between Turkey and Armenia would be subject to the arbitration of the President of the United States, specifically in the areas of Erqerum, Trebizond, Van, and Bitlis. Furthermore, President Wilson was given the role of arbitrating any access that Armenia might require to the sea and overseeing Turkish demilitarization along the Turkish borders with Armenia.

Although President Wilson was charged with helping to determine Armenia's borders with Turkey, the question of its borders with Azerbaijan and Georgia, the formerly Russian-controlled states along its northeastern frontier, were, in Article 92, left to "be determined by direct agreement between the States concerned." The Allies, however, reserved the right to step in if a agreement could not be reached.

SYRIA AND MESOPOTAMIA

The territory of Syria fell within the French area of influence, whereas Mesopotamia was to be overseen by the British forces that currently occupied it. Although Article 94 specified that both Syria and Mesopotamia would be "provisionally recognised as independent States," they were "subject to the rendering of administrative advice and assistance by a Mandatory [the French or British] until such time as they are able to stand alone."

The question of how the powers would determine whether the two countries were "able to stand alone," as well as precisely how long the mandates were designed to last, was not specified. The

British allies in Arabia clearly felt that they had been promised their own kingdoms in those two regions; Faysal had already seized Syria and was ruling it as its king, and his brother Abdullah planned to rule Mesopotamia in a similar fashion. The Treaty of Sèvres made no mention of Sharif Hussain's sons, however, or whether their authority was to be recognized in future.

A JEWISH HOMELAND

In addition to leaving open the specifics of self-rule in Syria and Mesopotamia, the seventh section of the Treaty of Sèvres addressed the question of Palestine and whether a Jewish homeland was to be established there. Article 95 specified that Palestine was also to become a mandated territory whose overseer would be selected by the Allies. Article 95 noted, however, that this authority

> ... will be responsible for putting into effect the declaration originally made on November 2, 1917, by the British Government, and adopted by the other Allied Powers, in favour of the establishment in Palestine of a national home for the Jewish people, it being clearly understood that nothing shall be done which may prejudice the civil and religious rights of existing non-Jewish communities in Palestine, or the rights and political status enjoyed by Jews in any other country.

This was an astonishingly sweeping statement, one that contradicted the earlier promise made by the British to Sharif Hussain that he would rule over all the Arabs. The needs and desires of the approximately 700,000 Arabic-speaking people in the region were not considered when their land was designated as the new homeland for the Jews. They believed that Palestine was too small and too barren for a second country to be created within it—that is, without effectively removing or exterminating the people who were already there.[19]

ARABIA

Although the promises made by the British to Sharif Hussain were neglected in regard to the majority of the land that he had

THE BALFOUR DECLARATION

On November 2, 1917, the British Foreign Secretary, Arthur James Balfour, wrote a letter to Lord Rothschild, a leader of the Jewish community in Great Britain. That letter, which would become known as "The Balfour Declaration," contained only three paragraphs, but within those three paragraphs was an explosive statement that would permanently alter international politics and the history of the modern Middle East.

In this letter was the first significant declaration by a world power in support of the creation of a national homeland for Jewish people in the territory known as Palestine. Lord Rothschild was a prominent Zionist, a supporter of the movement attempting to create a single, "national home" for Jews in Palestine, and Balfour's supportive letter represented a significant shift in British thinking about the region it had, in the Sykes-Picot Agreement, designated for international oversight.

The text of the letter was simple and straightforward:

Dear Lord Rothschild,

I have much pleasure in conveying to you, on behalf of His Majesty's Government, the following declaration of sympathy with Jewish Zionist aspirations which has been submitted to, and approved by, the Cabinet:

His Majesty's Government view with favour the establishment in Palestine of a national home for the Jewish people, and will use their best endeavours to facilitate the achievement of this object, it being clearly understood that nothing shall be done which may prejudice the civil and religious rights of existing non-Jewish communities in Palestine, or the rights and political status enjoyed by Jews in any other country.

I should be grateful if you would bring this declaration to the knowledge of the Zionist Federation.

Yours,
Arthur James Balfour

Source: www.bbc.co.uk

believed would be his, the Treaty of Sèvres did specify his portion of the Arabian Peninsula, the region known as the Hijaz (or Hedjaz), as being "free and independent." In Article 99, the treaty noted,

> In view of the sacred character attributed by Moslems of all countries to the cities and the Holy Places of Mecca and Medina, His Majesty the King of the Hedjaz undertakes to assure free and easy access thereto to Moslems of every country who desire to go there on pilgrimage or for any other religious object, and to respect and ensure respect for the pious foundations which are or may be established there by Moslems of any countries in accordance with the precepts of the law of the Koran.

The annual pilgrimage to the holy cities of Mecca and Medina was an important tenet of Islam. It was considered critical for all Muslims, at least once in their lives, to make this journey, and the revenue from this annual influx of pilgrims was a source of great wealth for Sharif Hussain. The treaty's attempt to impose restrictions on this critical aspect of his kingdom, while reneging on so many other promises, did little to endear the so-called King of the Hedjaz to his former allies, the British.

EGYPT, SUDAN, AND CYPRUS

Article 101 of the treaty specified that Turkey would renounce all claims to Egypt and further stated that Turkey's possession of Egypt would be backdated to go into effect as of November 5, 1914. It also noted that Turkey had to recognize the validity of the British protectorate over Egypt announced on December 18, 1914.

Male residents of Egypt over the age of 18 would be given the option, within a year, to choose whether they wished to become Egyptian or Turkish nationals. Husbands chose for their wives, and parents chose for their children under the age of 18. If they chose to identify themselves as Turkish rather than Egyptian, they were then required to move back to Turkish territory within one year. Furthermore, those who identified themselves as Egyptian received the bonus of British diplomatic protection.

A similar bonus awaited the residents of Sudan, formerly part of the Egyptian region and now a territory to be administered by Great Britain. When in foreign countries, Sudanese were to be given British diplomatic protection.

On November 5, 1914, the British government had announced its annexation of the island of Cyprus. The Treaty of Sèvres formalized this annexation and, in Article 117, noted, "Turkish nationals born or habitually resident in Cyprus will acquire British nationality and lose their Turkish nationality."

MOROCCO, TUNIS, LIBYA, AND THE AEGEAN ISLANDS

The stretch of the Ottoman Empire was also reduced in northern Africa and in the Aegean Sea. The treaty formalized the French protectorate in Morocco, backdating it to March 30, 1912, and noting that Moroccan goods entering Turkey were to be treated as French goods. The French protectorate in Tunis was also formalized and was backdated to go into effect as of May 12, 1881.

Libya was also formally separated from the Ottoman Empire, and its sultan—friendly to the Allied powers—was made ruler. Finally, Turkey was forced to renounce its claims over its islands in the Aegean Sea—Stampalia, Rhodes, Calki, Scarpanto, Casos, Pscopis, Misiros, Calymnos, Leros, Patmos, Lipsos, Sini, and Cos. These were to be granted to Italy.

A QUESTION OF FAITH

The caliph and ruler of the Ottoman Empire had been viewed by Muslims as a leader responsible for the protection and preservation of the holy cities of Mecca and Medina and as such the chief guardian of their faith's most important geography. The Treaty of Sèvres was meant to ensure that this power was stripped away, that those in Turkey did not attempt to influence those Muslims who were now living in different territories.

Article 139 required Turkey to renounce "all rights of suzerainty or jurisdiction of any kind over Moslems who are subject to the sovereignty or protectorate of any other State." This point was further emphasized, in startling language, in Article 142, which stated,

> ... in view of the terrorist régime which has existed in Turkey since November 1, 1914, conversions to Islam could not take place under normal conditions, no conversions since that date are recognised and all persons who were non-Moslems before November 1, 1914, will be considered as still remaining such, unless, after regaining their liberty, they voluntarily perform the necessary formalities for embracing the Islamic faith.

DISMANTLING THE EMPIRE

Beyond stripping away significant portions of Ottoman territory, the drafters of the Treaty of Sèvres clearly foresaw an opportunity to strip away any remaining power from Turkey. Part Five of the treaty required Turkey to demobilize within six months, to reduce its armed forces to a bare minimum—a few bodyguards for the sultan, a small police force to maintain order, and a small force to oversee Turkey's border controls. The total police presence was not to exceed 50,000 men, and their service had to be purely voluntary.

The amount of weapons available to this security force, as well as the supplies and vehicles or vessels they were able to use, was similarly specified in strictly controlled numbers. Any land within Turkey's borders that contained graves of Allied soldiers who were wounded or killed during the war was considered to belong to those Allied powers, not to Turkey.

The financial controls were perhaps the most crippling of all the blows dealt to Turkey. As specified in Article 231, Turkey was required to recognize "that by joining in the war of aggression which Germany and Austria-Hungary waged against the Allied Powers she has caused to the latter losses and sacrifices of all kinds for which she ought to make complete reparation." As a result, the Allied Powers decided to create a financial commission composed of one representative each from Great Britain, Italy, and France. This group would be responsible for complete oversight and approval of Turkey's finances—its budget, its economic planning, and the regulation of its currency. Furthermore, all of Turkey's revenues were to be placed under the control of the financial commission, which would use them to pay the Allied Powers for the cost of maintaining their troops in former Ottoman territories and for loss of people or property during the war. Only one representative from Turkey was to sit on the financial commission. Only the Allied powers would be allowed to hold the chairmanship of the commission, in rotation, and any vote would be decided by majority, effectively ensuring that Turkey would be outvoted in every decision.

The commission was given the right to visit and inspect any and all places in Turkey and to demand any "records, documents and information which it may require." It was given the right to control and collect taxes.

The "firm, just and durable Peace" that the Treaty of Sèvres claimed as its goal held little promise for the Ottoman Empire or its people. The people most affected—the residents of Turkey, Syria, Mesopotamia, Arabia, and Palestine and the Kurds and Armenians—found little to celebrate. Many of those who had hoped for the defeat of the Ottoman Empire were bitterly disappointed at what its defeat had brought. They had hoped for independence, for the right to govern themselves, and for their own homelands along the boundaries that they believed were fair and just.

The boundaries carved out by the Treaty of Sèvres, like the treaty itself, would prove short lived. The legacy that they left behind—of conflict, disappointment, and anger; of a determination to right perceived injustices and broken promises—would haunt the Middle East long after the Treaty of Sèvres had become little more than a footnote in history.

5

In Search
of Kurdistan

The Treaty of Sèvres imposed a new set of boundaries in the Middle East—arbitrary borders that carved up the Ottoman Empire not with a view to the needs and rights of its people but instead based on the political needs of the Allied powers who had proved victorious in World War I. Borders were created based on the desires of foreign powers to strengthen their positions in the region, to create new zones of influence, and to protect their economic and colonial interests.

Despite the complicated diplomacy that preceded it and the time and effort dedicated to its creation, the Treaty of Sèvres was never formally enforced. Its punitive terms and boundaries never went into effect and were soon replaced by other treaties and agreements. It is ironic that, despite its brief appearance in diplomatic history, its effects would prove far-reaching. The conflicts that the treaty would spawn would long outlive the treaty itself. Its arbitrary borders and boundaries would create flashpoints throughout the region, turn allies into enemies, and create a climate ripe for revolution.

Perhaps the greatest mistake embodied by the treaty and sparked by its drafters was the attempt to suggest a promise of self-government for many of the former citizens of the Ottoman Empire—a promise that the Allies had little clear intent to enact. History is full of examples of conflict sparked by the promise of self-government, and the Middle East proved no different. Disputes over borders inevitably increase when self-government enters the equation for some but not all the peoples of a region. In the Middle East, the Allies were unable or unwilling to respond promptly to the questions: When would autonomy go into effect? What form would the new government take? Who would be its leader? What role would religion play in the new country? When would military occupation end?

For years, the promises inherent in the Treaty of Sèvres would spark conflict, as various groups attempted to achieve what they believed had been promised: a nation of their own and the right to govern it themselves. In the end, frequently following a period of violence and bloodshed, most succeeded. One people,

An idyllic scene in Kurdistan, a country that existed only in the lines of the Treaty of Sèvres and the imagination of the Kurdish people. Nearly a century later the Kurdish people continue to pursue the dream of a homeland.

however, would forever be haunted by what had been promised in the treaty: the Kurds.

A LAND CALLED KURDISTAN

One of the greatest tragedies spawned by the Treaty of Sèvres was the broken promise of a homeland for the Kurds. The treaty had promised the Kurds a territory east of the Euphrates River, south of the newly defined southern boundary of Armenia, and north of the sketched-out frontier between Turkey, Syria, and Iraq (Mesopotamia). It was a poor patch of land, bereft of the more fertile and oil-rich regions that were predominantly Kurdish. Even that small stretch of land—a region to be known as Kurdistan—would be taken away.

The Kurds traditionally lived in the mountainous regions at the point where the borders of Turkey, Iraq, and Iran now meet.

Even today, there are small numbers of Kurds living in Syria, Lebanon, and other areas, but the heart of Kurdish territory has long been the rugged Zagros Mountains, running from southeastern Turkey into northern Iraq and on to eastern Iran.

Although this loose outline encompasses the region defined to be Kurdistan, contemporary maps show no mention of the name. In fact, even within the Kurdish population there are different dialects of language, different customs and beliefs, and different tribal alliances and rivalries. Yet the Kurds have long believed that they have more in common with each other than with any of the countries that claim them as native. The Treaty of Sèvres set them apart, promising them the right to a land of their own. The treaty's terms and the aftermath of World War I gave hope to many groups living within the Ottoman Empire that they would be given their own nations. The Kurdish people continue to struggle, however, nearly a century later, to achieve the promise made to them in the Treaty of Sèvres—a land of their own.

A BRIEF HISTORY

The argument that first favored the creation of Kurdistan was that there was a single group of people that could be identified as Kurds. These people claimed—and still claim—that they formed a distinct community. They pointed to geography as yet more evidence of their separate identity. Since the early part of the thirteenth century, the territory at the intersection of modern Turkey, Iraq, and Iran was known as Kurdistan. By the sixteenth century, when Kurds moved north and west onto the Anatolian plateau as a result of tribal migrations, the term "Kurdistan" had become more specific, referring to the authority of a group of Kurdish fiefs over the region. The term meant more than simply a geographical boundary, however. There was a distinct culture in the region known as Kurdistan—a culture that could be described as "Kurdish."

The Kurds speak a distinct Indo-European language, similar to Afghan or Persian in that it is derived from the Iranian language. Unlike the majority of Iranians, however, Kurds are Sunni Muslims, not Shiites (which are different branches of Islam separated by certain religious customs and practices and a different belief about who was the true successor to the prophet Muhammad).

This distinct Kurdish culture was retained for centuries as different invaders swept across the lands and instituted their cultures in neighboring regions. References to a separate people known as "Kurds" date back to A.D. 700.

The Kurdish people allied with the Ottoman Empire during the sixteenth century in the conflict between the Ottoman and Safavid (in Persia) empires, when a border was effectively drawn between Ottoman and Persian territories. The Ottomans promised the Kurdish tribal chiefs their own fiefdoms in exchange for their support and their assistance in policing the new borders. The fiefdoms were, for the most part, located along this border.

From this alliance, 15 main emirates (or kingdoms) were carved out. The Ottoman government granted certain families the right to rule these emirates, with one family member selected to serve as emir. Until the nineteenth century, these emirates would provide the basis of government in Kurdistan.

INTO THE EMPIRE

This system of emirates created a curious kind of division in Kurdistan. Kurdish culture developed independently; there was a clear distinction between Kurdistan and other parts of the empire. The emirs chosen were selected from those friendly to Ottoman interests and could be replaced if they proved too independent.

Even this semi-autonomous group of territories came to an end in the 1800s. Attempts within the Balkan states to achieve their independence had alarmed the Ottoman government, and it began to take steps to centralize all authority in Istanbul. As control was slowly pulled back to the central government, the emirs resisted, and revolts began to break out. Some emirs attempted to ally themselves with the Persian rulers; others attempted to declare the independence of their emirates. These attempts were quickly stamped out.

The result was a radical transformation of Kurdish authority. Ottoman representatives could not exercise the kind of specific and firm rule that the emirs had, particularly in settling internal disputes. Society within Kurdistan broke down into smaller units, as religious leaders and *aghas*—the old tribal chiefs— became the authorities in a single village or cluster of villages.

A religious leader named Sheikh Ubaydallah attempted to organize a revolt against the Ottomans in 1880. He appealed to the British for help in his effort to create an independent Kurdish region, writing to the British vice consul, "The Kurdish nation is a people apart. Their religion is different and their laws and customs are distinct."[20] This early attempt to establish an independent Kurdish state was soon stamped out.

When the Young Turks seized power in the early part of the twentieth century, the Kurdish leaders actively supported the political movement. They hoped that the Young Turks, in over-throwing Ottoman corruption, might also consider the demands for Kurdish nationalism. Kurdish clubs and journals began to appear, and some Kurdish language schools were founded.

Soon the ultra-nationalist ideals of the Young Turks clashed with Kurdish aspirations. To cement their control, the Young Turks closed all non-Turkish schools, clubs, and publications.

WORLD WAR I

When the Ottoman Empire went to war, many Kurds fought and died for their sultan. Russia—under the leadership of the tsar—took advantage of this period to make overtures to both the Armenians and the Kurds, promising to aid the Kurdish nationalist movement with supplies and funds. As a result, some Kurds joined the Russian side, either by fleeing over the border and into Russia or by switching sides and fighting with the Russians.

Russia, which had most likely intended to annex Kurdistan after the war, instead collapsed in revolution, and the new government declared invalid the agreements made by the tsar. The Kurds soon found themselves the victims of Ottoman persecution for their suspected role in aiding Russia. Many were driven from their homes along the northeastern front, forced to march westward in winter through rain and snow. Thousands died before the march ended.

ARBITRARY BORDERS

After the war's end and the collapse of the Ottoman Empire, the dream of an independent Kurdistan seemed possible. The Kurdish representatives were too weak and disorganized to seize the opportunity, however, and the other forces around the negotiating table had very specific aspirations for the region.

British forces had occupied the area of Mosul, in Iraqi Kurdistan, and had carried out enough studies to determine that the region was rich in oil. Earlier negotiations, including the Sykes-Picot Agreement, had promised the territory to France, but now Great Britain was determined to hold on to it. British representatives decided to enlist local support and met with Kurdish leaders, including General Sharif Pasha, who would serve as the head of the Kurdish delegation at the Paris Peace Conference. Pasha and the others were promised an independent or autonomous Kurdistan in exchange for siding with the British in their claim for Mosul.

France reluctantly agreed to a new Kurdish state; however, it exempted the Kurdish territories that bordered Syria and the region between Cilicia and the western bank of the Euphrates River. Great Britain had reserved Mosul, noting in the Treaty of Sèvres only that the residents of the oil-rich region would be consulted about whether they wanted to join Kurdistan. This could only have happened if Kurdistan had actually become independent and if the Allies had determined that the people were "capable of such independence."

The Treaty of Sèvres drew a series of hypothetical lines through Kurdish territory, separating traditional Kurdish lands from each other and cutting off areas with Kurdish majorities from the frontiers of what the treaty described as Kurdistan. The Kurdish people living west of the Euphrates, in the districts of Adiyaman, Darende, Divrik, Elbistan, and Malatya, were placed instead within the French "zone of interest." France also was granted oversight—through its Syrian mandate—of the Kurdish mountain area known as Kurd-Dagh, the Kurdish region of the Djasireh plain, and the Kurdish towns of Aintab, Biredjik, Djaziret ibn Omar, Kilis, Mardin, Nusaybin, and Urfa. In all, the Treaty of Sèvres allowed France to annex directly or indirectly approximately one-third of the territories that had been known as Kurdistan under the Ottoman Empire.

President Wilson had spoken out passionately in favor of the right of all people to self-determination, but these noble principles were overlooked at the time of the drafting of the Treaty of Sèvres. The treaty noted that the borders of Armenia would be determined by President Wilson and subject to his oversight and that Armenia would become a U.S. mandate. Without studying or consulting the local ethnic population, Wilson placed within the Armenian state several territories whose population was principally Kurdish—the regions of Bingol, Bitlis, Erzincan, Igdir, Erzurum, Karakilisa, Mus, and Van.[21] The arbitrary border deprived the Kurds of yet another third of the land that had been considered part of Kurdistan under the Ottomans.

The borders created by the Treaty of Sèvres left a Kurdistan that was merely a shadow of what the Kurds believed was rightfully theirs. They had been offered a Kurdish state, but a state that excluded two-thirds of traditional Kurdish territory. What remained was a much poorer land, creating an agricultural society missing its fertile territories and a culture of herdsmen lacking their traditional grazing areas.

The treaty essentially carved up Kurdish territory into five pieces. France would control the west and also (through Syria) the south; Persia was given the eastern region; Armenia was given the north. The Kurds were offered only the center, one-third of what they felt should rightfully constitute Kurdistan. The only economic asset that was left in the center was the oil-rich region of Mosul, but Mosul was a separate entity whose oil was to be controlled by the British.

The Treaty of Sèvres offered little to the Kurds. Events in Turkey and elsewhere soon made even these feeble promises invalid. Gradually, the dim outlines of Kurdistan would fade, swallowed up by the new nations of Turkey, Iraq, Iran, and Syria. The fading promises of the Treaty of Sèvres would remain sharp and vivid for the Kurds, who still viewed themselves as a real and separate group. Turkey, Iraq, Iran, and Syria would develop their own, very different political systems, which at times seemed to share only one common point of agreement: A separate Kurdistan should not and could not be created.

Tragically, nearly a century later, long after most of the world has forgotten the Treaty of Sèvres, the Kurds still remember. They point to the few articles that carved out a small portion of Kurdish territory as proof that they are entitled to a country of their own. The artificial and arbitrary borders placed by Allied leaders to mark off Kurdistan—a dim shadow of traditional Kurdish territory—have remained real for Kurdish nationalists. A document that was never enforced, and borders placed arbitrarily to serve foreign interests, continue to inspire Kurdish efforts to win the world's recognition of the boundaries of the territory they still call Kurdistan.

6

An Abandoned Cause

The brutal massacre of Armenians by the Ottoman forces had horrified people in the West, and Allied leaders made extensive use of the mistreatment of Armenians to mobilize public support for the war. The Armenians were alternately depicted as sad victims or as valiant resistors, bravely struggling against the oppressive Ottoman tyrants.

After World War I ended, the Armenians demanded what they believed had been promised them—a nation of their own. They were specific about the boundaries of the future "Armenia"—it would include eastern Anatolia, as well as portions of northern and central Anatolia, and Cilicia—the area surrounding the city of Adana. This, the Armenians believed, would provide them with access to the Mediterranean.

Their demands posed a problem as the Treaty of Sèvres was being finalized, because much of the territory that the Armenians wanted had already been promised to France in the Sykes-Picot Agreement. There were even greater problems with the Armenians' claim. In the territory that they were claiming, they had made up no more than 17 percent of the population *before* the war, a percentage that had decreased during the war years. A study by the British showed that the Armenian minority could not possibly control the territory unless they were supported by a foreign military of at least 100,000 men.[22]

This was a disastrous proposition for the Allied leaders, who all were under tremendous pressure to reduce their postwar military presence in the region, not increase it. The European Allies first informed the Armenians that the land that they were requesting was too big a territory. They might instead be allowed to take the territory that the Sykes-Picot Agreement had designated for Russia.

The final step for the European allies was to dispose of their part in the problem by making Armenia an American mandate and specifying, in the Treaty of Sèvres, that President Wilson would be responsible for setting the final boundaries of the future Armenian state.

ANCIENT CIVILIZATION

The struggles of the Armenians in the twentieth century stand in stark contrast to the rich Armenian culture that flourished thousands of years ago. The land defined as Armenia in ancient times was located in the high mountains north of Mesopotamia (Iraq) and Syria. Historical Armenia stretched from uplands west to the Armenian Plateau in eastern Anatolia and east to Azerbaijan and the Kurdish territory. At its largest, the area inhabited by ancient Armenian people occupied more than 100,000 square miles.[23]

Armenian territory is high and mountainous. The region contains Mount Ararat, believed to be the point where Noah's ark landed after its journey through 40 days and 40 nights of rain. The heart of Armenia was believed to be the Armenian Plateau in eastern Anatolia, lying between the Pontus Mountains in the north and the Taurus Mountains in the south. Historically, the very geographic features that defined Armenia—high mountains rising above the valleys of neighboring territories, rich in natural resources—made it a target for numerous invaders, who recognized the land's strategic positioning and the opportunity its topography offered for launching attacks on other territories in the lowlands. Those who controlled Armenia could control much of western Asia.

Invaders came from the west—Macedonian armies, Roman armies, Byzantine armies—and from the east—Persian armies, Turk armies, Mongol armies. They also came from the south—Selucid armies, Arab armies, Mamluk armies.

The ancient Armenians were one of the first people to develop metallurgy. They had arrived in the plateau region as conquerors themselves, from an Indo-European race. After being conquered by Achaemenids and Seleucids, they gained their independence and built an empire that ruled during the second and first centuries B.C.

The Armenians were then conquered by the Arsacids, who allowed the Armenians some limited self-government and introduced them to the practice of Christianity. It became the state religion around A.D. 301. A century later, the Armenians adopted their own alphabet, and Armenian literature quickly began to flourish.[24]

Armenia was subjected first to Persian and Byzantine rule and then was conquered by Arabs. A brief period of self-rule followed, extinguished by another Byzantine conquest and then invasion by Turks. Self-government lingered a bit longer in Cilicia. There, an Armenian principality was declared in 1080, and, approximately 100 years later, an Armenian kingdom was established. The Christian heritage remained strong in Cilicia, whose rulers built alliances with the European Crusaders. In the fourteenth century, Cilicia was invaded by Mamluk forces from Egypt. Frantic messages requesting European assistance were ignored. The period of independence for Armenia finally came to an end.

OTTOMAN RULE

In the sixteenth and seventeenth centuries, the Armenian plateau was a flashpoint for warring Ottoman and Persian forces as they battled for supremacy. The Ottomans first won the western and central portions of the plateau, and, after nearly 100 more years of conflict, they won the remaining Armenian territory.

By the nineteenth century, Russia had emerged as a powerful neighbor. At first, Russian armies invaded through the Caucasus Mountains and seized the Persian territories north of the Araxes River. Later, they won additional territory from the Ottomans, creating a transcaucasian region that stretched from the Caspian Sea to the Black Sea. Russian victories inspired the Armenians to reconsider their status as a distant outpost in the Ottoman Empire. Soon, representatives from Armenia were secretly meeting with the Russians, pleading with the tsar to help liberate Armenia. There was a religious element to this alliance; both Russia and Armenia were predominantly Christian, whereas the Ottoman Empire was the guardian of Islam.

War pitted Russia against the Ottoman forces from 1877 to 1878, and Russia added additional portions of the Armenian

Plateau to its transcaucasian territory. Initially, Armenians (many of whom had fought with the Russians) were promised that the Russian troops would remain in the plateau until the Ottoman sultan had carried out reforms to protect the Armenians. In a tragic foreshadowing of later events, however, the promise was broken, and Russian troops evacuated the region.

The Armenian desire for nationalism, encouraged by Russia, was not so easily stamped out. By 1894, the Ottoman sultan was increasingly worried by the Armenian nationalist movement and conflicts between the Armenians and the Kurds. To help unify his empire, he encouraged a renewed focus on sharia (Islamic law). Many of his followers took the emphasis on Islam to mean that any other religions should be suppressed. From 1894 to 1896, thousands of Armenian Christians were massacred, yet another foreshadowing of the violence that would arise only a few decades later. Estimates vary on precisely how many Armenians were murdered, but between 2 and 12 percent of the Armenian population (50,000 to 300,000 people) were killed during the massacres.[25] Larger numbers of Muslims were relocated to the region.

THE WAR

When World War I broke out, the Ottoman Empire's surprise attack on Russia presented a conflict to the Armenians. Some had placed their hopes in the sultan, others in the Young Turks. Russia had once more been fanning the flames of Armenian nationalism. As in so many cases in the Middle East, the superpowers were quite adept at encouraging nationalist aspirations as a way to weaken the Ottoman Empire and ultimately expand their own influence in the region.

As described previously, the actions of some Armenians who chose to collaborate with the Russians brought disaster to the region. Thousands were massacred, and thousands more were deported from the territory. A document from the Ottoman Ministry of the Interior, dated August 29, 1915, makes clear the apparent reason:

These Greek and Armenian refugee children were photographed in 1923 at a barracks near Athens, Greece, after huge numbers of families were dislocated by the hostilities between the Armenians and the Turks.

> The government's goal in taking Armenians from their places of residence and sending them to selected places of settlement is to ensure that this element will be prevented from engaging in activities against the government and that it will become incapable of pursuing its national goals regarding the establishment of an Armenian Government.[26]

THE TREATY

As it became clear in the aftermath of the war that Armenia was interested in establishing its own nation—a hope encouraged by the Allies—Turkish newspapers began emphasizing the close ties between Armenia and Turkey:

The Armenian Republic owes its establishment to Turkey. The present Armenian politicians should keep in mind that the Tsarist Russia which was our worst enemy until very recently attempted to incite Armenians to rebellion and to thus establish an Armenian State against the vital interests of Turkey. Armenian-Turkish hostilities have disappeared, and it can be said that a regime of Turkish-Armenian friendship is blooming now in our country.... No matter how (international) political events may develop, Turkish Armenians should never lose sight of the fact that their fate is united with that of the Turks. Their political existence can be assured by being one of the Ottoman elements. There is no sense in expecting any benefit from the intervention of any foreign state.[27]

The Armenians were expecting a benefit from the help of foreign allies, however. In this, they would be disappointed.

The question of how to handle Armenia had been placed in the hands of the United States. President Wilson had supported the idea of an American mandate in Armenia. In part, this was in response to a growing awareness of the strategic importance of the Middle East. It was also in response to the active lobbying of American Christian missionaries, who viewed with horror the stories of Armenian massacres and wanted to preserve this Christian community.

Wilson commissioned an investigation of the region in August 1919, ultimately learning that Armenians were not in the majority in the territory designated by the Treaty of Sèvres as the future Armenia, nor had they been before the war. He learned that the brutal massacres of Armenians had, in part, been triggered by foreign involvement in the region, and that the region seemed clearly Turkish—in population, in architecture, and in many other important respects.

This did not change Wilson's mind, but it deeply affected the Congress, which was charged with approving the idea of an American mandate. The Senate and the country were increasingly isolationist in mood, and there was little support for

America's assuming a mandate that would require policing by 100,000 American soldiers to ensure the rule of a minority.

Soon, the philosophy among the Allies shifted. Rather than supporting the idea that Armenia must have foreign troops to survive, the powers now agreed that Armenia could be fully self-sufficient, supported only by a minor grant of supplies, once its borders had been set. The Armenian delegates agreed, fearing that if they did not, they might not get any land at all. President Wilson quickly drew up a set of borders for Armenia in November 1920. These borders did not reflect the population, the politics, or the power in the region. They were simply lines placed on a map, designed to extract President Wilson, the United States, and the Allied powers quickly from any responsibility for maintaining the peace in Armenia.

Shortly after President Wilson provided the Armenians with the outlines for their new state, the question of an independent Armenia was finally settled. Turkish and Bolshevik (Russian) forces swept into the region. The Armenians were quickly defeated, their territory was divided, and the republic of Armenia ceased to exist.

7

One Land Divided

The Treaty of Sèvres included the Balfour Declaration, which promised British support for the creation of a Jewish homeland in Palestine. The mandate for Palestine was granted to Great Britain, which through the Balfour Declaration had announced its recognition of the rights of Jews as a separate entity. At the same time, in the Balfour Declaration, the British government had promised, "nothing shall be done which may prejudice the civil and religious rights of the existing non-Jewish communities in Palestine."

Of all of the declarations in the Treaty of Sèvres, the formalization of the plan to create a homeland for Jews in Palestine has perhaps proved the most contentious. The divisions sparked between Jewish and Muslim communities, both in Palestine and worldwide, by these steps had an impact immediately and continue to reverberate to this day. The question of a group's "right" to a homeland, regardless of who is currently occupying that territory, is certainly not unique to the Middle East. The issue of arbitrary borders is debated to this day in the land we know now as Israel, as artificial borders continually reshape the divisions between Israeli and Palestinian territory.

When the British first occupied Palestine in 1917–1918, the region was devastated by famine, disease, and economic collapse, much of it related to World War I. The population of the region was approximately 650,000, of whom 55,000 were Jewish.[28] By 1947, the population had grown to 1,269,000 people, of whom one-third were Jewish.[29] Today, the population of the region, which now encompasses the state of Israel, contains more than six million people, of whom 80 percent are Jewish.[30]

A BRIEF HISTORY

Both Jews and Palestinians cite ancient ties to the land they claim, and both claims are historically accurate. Before the land was known as Israel or Palestine, it was called Canaan. The Canaanites were a Semitic people who traveled northwest from their homes in northern Mesopotamia (Iraq) and Syria and settled in the region. They eventually controlled all of Palestine west of the Jordan River and parts of coastal Lebanon (then called Phoenicia) and southern Syria. The land then known as Canaan gave the world an important cultural milestone: It was the Canaanites who first developed a linear alphabet, which (after being transmitted to the Greeks) became the basis for our Western system of writing.

For nearly 1,500 years, Canaanites controlled the region. The Canaanites brought their language to the territory—a Semitic language, of which Hebrew was one dialect.

In the twelfth century B.C., at nearly the same time, two groups entered Canaan. One group was known as *"Bnei Israel,"* or the Tribe of Israel. They were Jewish, marked by their belief in one God—a God who had brought them to this land—and they settled in the hilly region in Canaan's interior. The second group was the Philistines, Greeks who settled along Canaan's coastal plains.

It was not until the fifth century B.C. that the region was described as Palestine (a reference to the Philistine inhabitants) in the writings of Herodotus, a Greek historian.[31] Ultimately, the groups came into conflict over the land, and the Jewish people defeated the Canaanites and Philistines, establishing the Kingdom of Israel in approximately 1000 B.C.

Under its second king, King David, the kingdom of Israel grew, as the city of Jerusalem was captured and transformed into a holy site for Jews and territories were added in the north (through much of Syria) and to the Euphrates River. The kingdom lasted only 70 years, separating into two divisions following the death of David's son, King Solomon. This created the ten tribes of Israel (in the north) and Judah (containing Jerusalem) in the south. In 722 B.C., Israel was conquered by the Assyrians; in 586 B.C. Judah was conquered by the Babylonian Empire (which had succeeded the Assyrian rule in Mesopotamia).

The region of Palestine is generally thought to contain the kingdoms of Israel and Judah as they existed around 860 B.C.[32] This sets the borders of Palestine as follows: to the north, just beyond the eastern edge of the Dead Sea to the foot of the Golan; to the west, from the base of the Golan Heights to the

Mediterranean Sea; to the south, stretching to Gaza, bordering the Sinai Peninsula; and to the northern tip of the Gulf of Aqaba.

EMPIRES AND CONQUEST

The region was subject to conquest for many centuries. The Babylonian conquerors were replaced by Persian conquerors (the Achaemenids) in 539 B.C. A Jewish revolt in 140 B.C. (when the temple in Jerusalem—the holiest site in the Jewish faith—was dedicated to the Greek god Zeus) led to a brief period of independence, which lasted about 80 years. Soon the Roman Empire swept into the Middle East. By 63 B.C., Palestine (then called Judea) had become another piece of the vast Roman Empire.

Under Roman rule, Jews in Palestine were granted a certain amount of autonomy. A revolt from A.D. 132 to 135 was met with a fierce Roman response, and the region (no longer autonomous) became the Roman colony of Syria Palestina. Soon, there were greater numbers of Jews living outside Palestine than within its borders. Although under stricter Roman laws the Jews were forbidden to enter Jerusalem, it remained the holiest site in the Jewish faith.

In the seventh century, Palestine was conquered by Arab invaders. This invasion, and the conquest of much of the Middle East, had been led by followers of the prophet Muhammad, who lived from 570 to 632 B.C. Born in Mecca (in the region now known as Saudi Arabia), Muhammad established in Medina a community of followers who believed that he had been chosen to preach God's word. His teachings formed the basis of a new faith known as Islam.

The faith soon spread beyond the Arabian Peninsula, as Muslims conquered Mesopotamia, western Iran, Syria, and Palestine. Within 100 years of Muhammad's death, his followers had carved out an empire that extended from the Pyrenees Mountains in Europe to the Indus River basin in India.

Although Palestine played a relatively minor role in this Islamic empire, it did contain one important site—Jerusalem. Along with Mecca and Medina, Jerusalem is one of the three holy cities of Islam. In Islamic belief, Muhammad stopped briefly in Jerusalem during his journey to heaven. The place where he stopped is the Temple Mount—the site of the holy Jewish temple. In 691 B.C., a shrine was placed over the stone, known as the Dome of the Rock.

Muslims soon formed a majority of the population in Palestine, but Jews and Christians lived there, too. All groups lived in relative harmony and were allowed to practice their respective faiths. This came to an end in 1099, when Crusaders invaded Jerusalem, stamping out any non-Christian expression of faith and brutally forcing Jews and Muslims out.

Less than 100 years later, the Muslim leader Saladin reconquered Jerusalem. Apart from a few brief revolts, Palestine was ruled by Muslim leaders until the twentieth century and by Ottoman Turks from 1516 until 1918.

AN EMPIRE'S COLLAPSE

Apart from Jerusalem, Palestine was of little interest to Ottoman rulers. The land was never extensively settled, nor were serious attempts made to assimilate it into the empire. It was rugged terrain, and when the empire began to decline, Palestine was largely neglected.

The land was undeveloped but not uninhabited. Palestinian Arab communities were spread throughout the territory, in both urban and rural areas. Small Jewish communities lived in Jerusalem, Hebron, and Safed, as well as in the rural areas in agricultural clusters. In the late nineteenth and early twentieth centuries, European influence in the region grew. Europeans and Americans sent missionary groups. The territory began to develop economically, exporting wheat, cotton, olives and olive oil, and citrus fruit. Western goods were imported. Divisions began to increase between the wealthy landowners (who lived in the cities) and the laborers.

It is interesting to note that the first concern about increased Jewish settlement in Palestine came not from Muslims but from Christians. In 1899, Catholic priest Father Henry Lammens

The Zionist movement was launched at the end of the nineteenth century to create a permanent Jewish homeland. These members of the Zionist Commission arrive in Palestine in April 1918 to promote the idea of locating the Jewish state there.

published a newspaper article asking the Ottoman regime to prevent or restrict Jewish colonization in Palestine.[33]

The Zionist movement was launched to create a permanent Jewish homeland, and initially the Ottoman sultan seemed amenable to allowing it to be placed in Palestine. The Ottoman Empire was in economic crisis. Representatives of the Zionist cause met with the sultan, offering a substantial amount of cash in exchange for territory that, at one point, was to stretch from Haifa and Akka to the Transjordan and the Dead Sea.[34]

In the early 1900s, substantial amounts of land in Palestine were bought by Jewish immigrants. These new immigrants arrived in the region between 1900 and 1914. They wanted to build a separate Jewish society focusing on the land; their philosophy was socialist and their vision relied on agricultural development. They envisioned a stretch of land developed and owned by Jews and Jews alone. These Jewish immigrants were more European in their clothing and more socialist in their ideals, and they brought a new perspective and philosophy to the more Middle Eastern Jewish society that had traditionally existed in Palestine.

THE WAR AND ITS AFTERMATH

As discussed previously, even before World War I ended, the Allied powers were carving up Ottoman territories through agreements and treaties, focusing on competition with each other as much as elimination of Ottoman influence in the region. Great Britain viewed Palestine in strategic terms as a critical buffer between French-held territory and the valuable Suez Canal, controlled by Great Britain in Egypt.

This led, at first, to plans for international oversight of Palestine, with British enclaves remaining in the region. Later, a strong Zionist community in Palestine, presumably friendly to British interests, proved just as attractive.

This, of course, reneged on a separate British agreement with Sharif Hussain of the Hijaz region in Arabia, who had been promised to be made king of all Arabs in exchange for encouraging an Arab revolt against Ottoman rule. Precisely what his kingdom would include (and exclude) became the subject of intense argument after the war. Correspondence between Sharif Hussain and the British High Commissioner in Mecca, Sir Henry McMahon, reflected this confusion. In a letter to McMahon on July 14, 1915, Hussain claimed for "the Arab nation" independence for a vast territory whose boundaries included all of Syria, Palestine, Lebanon, Iraq, and the Arabian Peninsula.[35]

After many letters back and forth, McMahon exempted certain specific areas from the proposed Arab kingdom, including Baghdad and Basra in Iraq and portions of Syria. The areas were deliberately vague, but Hussain believed that Palestine would be included in his kingdom. He felt that the terms of the Treaty of Sèvres—including the references to Palestine—clearly violated what he had been promised.

THE TREATY

At the Paris Peace Conference, the delegation representing the Zionist movement extensively lobbied for official recognition of Palestine as the Jewish homeland, where Jews would operate more or less autonomously. These delegates further specified

GERTRUDE BELL

In the period after World War I, most treaties and agreements signed by Europeans reflected the belief that the Middle East's future depended on European oversight. One key member of the British intelligence service, however, believed that Arab rule was the key to the region. Her name was Gertrude Bell.

Bell was a courageous and accomplished British traveler, described by the people she met on her journeys as the "Desert Queen." She was among the earliest women to attend Oxford University and became a skilled mountain climber, linguist, and published author.

Bell felt most at home in the Middle East, studying its languages and learning the customs, spending time in Persia (now Iran), Arabia, and Mesopotamia (Iraq). Unlike many Europeans, she preferred to travel alone, hiring native guides and then setting out into the desert sands, gaining a vast understanding of the people and customs that shaped the region.

Her knowledge proved invaluable to Great Britain during World War I, when Bell was asked by British officials to help gather intelligence. She provided valuable information to the war effort in Cairo and then was transferred to Mesopotamia.

Bell formed alliances with many influential Arabs, including Faysal, the future king of Iraq. She helped shape the kingdom that Faysal was granted, assisting in mapmaking to mark the borders of Iraq, and was one of his closest aides when he first was crowned king. She founded the Iraqi museum, helped oversee archeological digs so that Iraq's rich antiquities were preserved and retained, and sketched out the design for its flag.

The king and his people did not wish to be guided by the British through the process of governing their own country, however. They wanted to shape their own destiny, and that would require full independence. Recognizing that her role in her beloved adopted country was fading, Bell committed suicide in 1926. The kingdom she helped build would outlast her by only 12 years.

that the boundaries of Palestine would include southern Lebanon up to and including the Litani River, the east bank of the Jordan, and the Sinai Peninsula.[36]

President Wilson sent a delegation to parts of the Middle East, including Palestine, to survey the inhabitants and determine how they wished to be governed. This delegation—the King-Crane Commission—spoke with both Arabs and Jews in Palestine and returned with the recommendation that the Zionist expansion in Palestine should be curtailed and a single Arab state of Greater Syria (including Palestine and Lebanon) should be created. Sharif Hussain's son Faysal would serve as its king, and the mandatory power in the region should be the United States or (as second choice) Great Britain. In nearly every respect, save the second choice of mandatory power, these recommendations were ignored. The best interests of the citizens of the Ottoman Empire had had little influence on the decisions made in carving up the Middle East. It was the best interests of the Allied leaders that had more weight in the decision about where new borders would be placed.

A LAST LOOK

Although the Treaty of Sèvres never went into effect, its validation of the Balfour Declaration set the region of Palestine on a path of inevitable conflict between Jewish and Arab inhabitants. Great Britain's commitment to establish a Jewish homeland in Palestine—a commitment that ultimately supported Jewish domination of the territory—was made without regard for the wishes of those who made up the majority of the population. Instead, it was made to ensure a friendly presence in the region and a buffer between French territory and British territory.

In Palestine, perhaps more than in any other part of the Middle East, the true motives of those who drafted the Treaty of Sèvres are clearly reflected. Decisions were made for strategic reasons without thought of their impact on the region's inhabitants. Borders were drawn to satisfy French and British aspirations in the region, not to encourage autonomy or independence. The drafters of the Treaty of Sèvres felt that the lands of the Middle East were theirs to divide; they focused only on gaining the consent of each other rather than of those who lived there.

The Treaty of Sèvres was intended to settle the question of who would control the Middle East. It was supposed to mark an end to the conflict that had culminated in World War I. For the Palestinian Arabs and Jews, however, it marked not a conflict's end but its beginning.

8

Divisions and Destiny

The boundaries carved out by the Treaty of Sèvres often ignored the realities of history and population statistics, focusing more on the aims and desires of the superpowers. Greece provided one of the greatest blind spots in the treaty. Greece had not fought against Ottoman forces on a significant scale during World War I. At the Paris Peace Conference, however, Greece produced a set of documents that were claimed to support its postwar claim to southern Albania, all of Thrace, all of the Aegean Islands (including the Dodecanese, which Italy had been promised and was occupying), the British colony of Cyprus, and a substantial portion of southwestern Anatolia.

The Greek claim was based on the fact that all these territories had been ruled by Greeks at some point in time. Only Cyprus and the other islands had a population whose majority was Greek; Greeks had formed just a small minority in the other territories for thousands of years.[37]

British Prime Minister David Lloyd George was a strong supporter of the Greeks and ignored the statistics produced by his own war office and foreign office, which showed that in southern Albania, eastern Thrace, and southwestern Anatolia—all areas claimed by Greece—the majority of the population was Muslim.[38] He believed that a strong Greek presence would protect British interests in the eastern Mediterranean. Reserving only British-held Cyprus, he agreed to the rest of Greek demands. President Wilson also ignored his experts' recommendations and supported Greece's claims.

Greece was authorized by the Allies to occupy the port city of Izmir in Western Anatolia, directly across the Aegean Sea from Greece. This authority was given in May 1919, well before the Treaty of Sèvres was signed. The official reason for this was that Greeks were being massacred, but in fact this was not true. Instead, the hope was that a Greek presence in the region would prevent Italy from claiming the land.

Greek forces landed at Izmir on May 15, 1919, and immediately began killing Turkish civilians and officials of the Ottoman government. The Greeks continued the massacres, pushing well beyond the area that they had been authorized to occupy. Both France and Italy quickly demanded that Greek actions in Anatolia be investigated. A commission was dispatched to Anatolia. The commission reported back that there had been no initial massacre of the Greek population, so the Greek occupation was not justified. In addition, the report once more confirmed that the majority of the region's population was Muslim.

Ignoring this report, David Lloyd George continued to support Greek claims, even as Greek forces marched on into Thrace and western Anatolia. In the Treaty of Sèvres, Izmir and its surrounding territory were placed under Greek administration. A vote was to be held in five years to determine whether Greece would annex the territory. Greece was also given eastern Thrace, a territory that placed Greek forces within only a few miles of the Ottoman capital of Istanbul.

PRIDE AND PREJUDICE

On August 10, 1920, the Treaty of Sèvres was signed. Its terms for foreign occupation of former Ottoman territories, dividing lands between Greece, Great Britain, France, and Italy and creating a patchwork of independent states, "zones of interest," and mandated territories, are a stunning display of the arrogance of the victorious Allies. The Treaty of Sèvres left the remnants of the Ottoman Empire humiliated—and its citizens angry and desperate.

Those in Turkey who read the terms of the treaty could see what the future might bring. The Ottoman Empire was no more; Turkey was left with only northwest and north central Anatolia, plus the city of Istanbul. Greek forces could be stationed close enough to shoot cannons at the city, so most likely Istanbul would also be eventually lost, because the Treaty of Sèvres dictated that the Ottoman Empire, now reduced to Turkey alone, could not have an army or navy to defend its capital or its country.

The Treaty of Sèvres was never enforced because an armed force of Turkish resistors refused to accept it. For this, the Treaty of Sèvres marked yet another milestone in Turkish history: Its harsh terms inspired Turks to unite around a new cause—saving their nation from extinction.

The resistance began with the C.U.P., whose leadership fled Istanbul and scattered, organizing cells of resistance just as they had in the days of the Ottoman sultan, before the revolution. Rather than disarm, members of the Ottoman armed forces melted away, often taking their weapons with them. In other instances, when weapons were thrown down, they later disappeared before they could be claimed by Allied forces.

The Ottoman army did begin to pull back from the borders drafted by the Treaty of Sèvres. The Armenians moved into southern and eastern Anatolia. French forces also moved into Anatolia, allying themselves with the Armenians as they claimed part of Anatolia for the northern territory of Syria. Italian forces landed to the south, claiming Antalya and Knoya.

It was not these actions but the Greek forces' seizure of Izmir that reinvigorated Turkish resistance. There was a long-standing animosity between Turks and Greeks dating back to the Balkan Wars. Western Anatolia, although not an actual site of combat, had suffered through the war. Its people were starving, and the war effort had claimed its men and supplies. Refugees from eastern Anatolia and the Balkans had come into the region during the war. Now, as Greeks rushed into the region, the crowds of refugees were joined by evicted Muslims. In all, estimates show that 1.2 million individuals became refugees as a result of the Greek invasion.[39]

The Turkish resistance began in several locations, but it coalesced under the leadership of the military leader Mustafa Kemal. Kemal had been a hero during the siege at Gallipoli and had helped defeat Russian forces on the eastern borders. After the war, the Ottoman government appointed him inspector-general of Ottoman forces in northern Anatolia. He immediately traveled to Samsun in Anatolia and organized armed resistance, forming the Turkish Nationalist Organization.

Kemal was as brilliant a politician as a military man, and he brought together soldiers, religious leaders, politicians, businessmen, and property owners. He presented them with a purpose—to preserve an independent Turkey—and a plan to carry it out.

Armed resistance was organized in Cilicia, where Muslims were being attacked and murdered by Armenians. The Armenians

ATATÜRK

The nation we know today as Turkey reflects little of its past as the aging center of a defeated Ottoman Empire. The Treaty of Sèvres was intended to crush any control that the Ottoman sultans still retained over the rest of their empire, but its terms would also have spelled the extinction of Turkey itself.

One man changed all of this, almost single-handedly. Mustafa Kemal, a respected military officer, united different groups under a single, unifying label—"Turks"—and inspired them to fight against the Allies to preserve their country, their culture, and their independence.

The result was triumph for the Turkish Nationalist forces under Kemal and the replacement of the oppressive Treaty of Sèvres with the Treaty of Lausanne. Mustafa Kemal did not stop there, however. Elected president of the new republic of Turkey, he oversaw the end of the sultanate, the end of the caliphate, and the elimination of all traces of Ottoman rule. In its place, Kemal began to build a modern, Western society, with an educated citizenry and women as well as men working together to build a more progressive Turkey.

Kemal's reforms were dramatic and extensive. He outlawed the wearing of the fez, the traditional Turkish hat. Women were discouraged from wearing the veil. The Christian calendar was adopted, using dates based on the Christian system of measuring time before and after Christ's death (B.C. and A.D.), as well as the 24-hour measurement of daily time popular in Europe. Muslims were allowed to marry non-Muslims, and all adults were granted the legal right to change religions if they wished. Turkey's government was defined as secular, rather than religious. A new alphabet was introduced, one based on Latin (as in Western languages) rather than Arabic letters—the use of the familiar Arabic alphabet was outlawed.

Mustafa Kemal served as Turkey's president for 15 years. His policies reshaped Turkey into a modern, strong nation, and even before his death he was widely hailed as Atatürk, the "Father of all Turks."

were at first supported by France. For nearly a year, fierce fighting ravaged the region. Villages were destroyed.

Finally, on October 21, 1921, France admitted defeat. It signed a treaty with the Turks, agreeing to give up its claims to Anatolia— in essence abandoning the Armenians to focus on Syria. France's decision marked a significant break among the Allies.

Armenians also fought with Turkish forces in eastern Anatolia and Transcaucasia. Here, Armenians controlled the urban areas and the rural parts of the plains, and Kurdish fighters and Muslim refugees controlled the mountains. As discussed previously, the Armenians were a minority in the territory that they had been given. Had the Allies kept their initial promise to provide a military presence of 100,000 soldiers, the Armenians might have held on to their territory. As it was, however, the Armenians were little match for the Turks sweeping in from the south. Worse still, they were also under attack from the north, this time by Russian forces that claimed the Armenian Republic as Russian territory.

On December 3, 1920, the Armenians signed a peace treaty with Turkish forces. In this Treaty of Alexandropol, they gave up their claim to eastern Anatolia. Shortly after the treaty was signed, the remaining Armenian territory was captured by Soviet (Russian) forces. The Soviets agreed to the Treaty of Alexandropol's borders, claiming the rest of Armenia for the Soviet Union.

WAR BETWEEN GREECE AND TURKEY

As Turkish forces won victories in Cilicia and the East, support for the Nationalist movement grew. Troops soon were concentrated in the west to battle Greek forces. On March 16, 1921, the Turkish Nationalists signed a treaty with the Soviet Union that provided the Turkish resistance with weapons and money.

In the summer of 1921, Greek forces had advanced to a point near Ankara. The noise of cannon shelling could be heard in Istanbul. The Turkish National Assembly, which previously had feared that Kemal was overly ambitious and power-hungry,

By the time this picture was taken in 1922, Turkish general and statesman Mustafa Kemal was commander in chief of the Turkish armed forces. He is shown here reviewing his troops during the war against Greece.

abruptly changed its mind as the panic of a potential invasion of their capital set in. They appointed Mustafa Kemal as commander-in-chief of the Turkish armed forces, granting him full authority.

Fighting continued for a year, until the Turks were able to beat back the Greek forces and advance into western Anatolia. By September 1922, the fighting finally came to an end.

The final focus was Greek occupation of eastern Thrace. As the Turkish military mobilized to attack, Greece pleaded with Great Britain for assistance. Great Britain apparently was beginning to understand the forces that the Treaty of Sèvres had unleashed and urged the Greeks to give up eastern Thrace. They reluctantly agreed.

On October 11, 1922, an armistice was signed between the British and the Turkish Nationalist forces. On October 2, 1923, British forces pulled out of Istanbul following the signing of the Treaty of Lausanne, the treaty that ultimately replaced the Treaty of Sèvres.

AN EXPENSIVE PEACE

The Ottoman Empire, despite its excesses and corruption, had been a multicultural society, with many different religious and ethnic groups unified into a single entity. The Treaty of Sèvres brought that to an end, splitting an empire containing many languages, cultures, and beliefs into fragments. The effect was both swift and long lasting. With the native population's understanding that a particular region was to become autonomous, conflicts quickly broke out between majority and minority groups over who would control the new state and what form that control would take.

The question of borders, which had existed only in the most basic form within the Ottoman Empire as separate *vilayets*, or administrative regions, now became vitally important. Where once parts of the Ottoman Empire had been colloquially known as Kurdistan or Armenia, the question of precisely where those boundaries began and ended became critical when autonomy was offered.

It is tragic that the Allies, as they drafted the Treaty of Sèvres, never understood precisely the mark that these divisions would leave on the Middle East. Years later, British Prime Minister David Lloyd George wrote in his *Memoirs of the Peace Conference* that critics of the postwar peace treaties simply did not understand them:

> As the World War of 1914–18 was the greatest clash of arms between nations ever waged on this earth, so was the Treaty of Versailles (with the ancillary Treaties of St. Germain, Trianon, Neuilly, and Sèvres) the most far-reaching and comprehensive settlement ever effected in any international dispute. It was inevitable that so colossal a readjustment of national boundaries in four continents and of international relations in five continents, where feuds have been fought out between races for countless years, should be provocative of controversy and be responsible for a complication of misunderstandings. It will be many generations before the world settles

down to a calm appreciation of the merits and demerits of the terms of these revolutionary compacts.[40]

Robert Lansing, the American secretary of state during the initial phase of the peace negotiations, later wrote of his dismay at the postwar division of the Ottoman territories through mandates and President Wilson's refusal to stop it: "If the advocates of the system intended to avoid through its operation the appearance of taking enemy territory as the spoils of war, it was a subterfuge which deceived no one."[41]

Lansing became so disappointed with Allied actions during the framing of the peace treaties, and in particular with President Wilson's decisions, that he resigned in February 1920 and published his own memoir of the peace negotiations shortly after. He noted:

> In the tentative distribution of mandates among the Powers, which took place on the strong assumptions that the mandatory system would be adopted, the principal European Powers appeared to be willing and even eager to become mandatories over territories possessing natural resources which could be profitably developed and showed an unwillingness to accept mandates for territories which, barren of mineral of agricultural wealth, would be continuous liabilities rather than assets.[42]

It is in this, then, that the greatest fault of the Treaty of Sèvres is found. The borders that it drew, the artificial boundaries that it drafted, were placed for the benefit of the Allies and to humiliate and subjugate the Ottoman Empire. Although the Treaty of Sèvres could not be enforced, its legacy is a Middle East where arbitrary borders are still fiercely contested; a people who nearly a century later regard Western actions with suspicion and anger; and a region where religious conflict continues to reshape a land where Muslims, Jews, and Christians once lived in peace.

9

A Legacy
of Conflict

The armistice that British forces had signed with Turkey on October 11, 1922—the Armistice of Mudanya—called for a renegotiation of the terms of the Treaty of Sèvres. On October 27, 1922, invitations were issued to attend a peace conference with this aim, a peace conference that was to be held in Lausanne, France. There were at this point two separate groups claiming to represent Turkey: the Turkish Nationalists, led by Mustafa Kemal, who had established a government based in Ankara, and the government of the sultan, based in Istanbul. Two separate invitations to attend the conference at Lausanne were issued to the two different Turkish governments, but it quickly became clear that only one could be the true and official representative of Turkey's interests.

Mustafa Kemal had been responsible for Turkey's victories against the Allies and had brought together a coalition of many different groups to preserve Turkey from extinction. The sultan, on the other hand, had been willing to negotiate with the Allies to preserve his office, and it was representatives of the sultan who had signed the Treaty of Sèvres and agreed to its oppressive terms. When it came time to choose one group to renegotiate with the Allies, most chose to back Mustafa Kemal.

The Turkish National Assembly, at Kemal's urging, put the matter to a vote on November 1, 1922. The assembly passed new legislation that officially separated religion and politics in Turkey. No more would Turkey's sultan also serve as *caliph* (the chief representative of Islam). With the new law, the caliphate and the sultanate were officially separated, and the sultanate was abolished.

The sultan at that time, Mehmet VI, the last sultan of Turkey, the thirty-sixth in a line of Ottoman rulers who had governed spiritual and political life in Turkey for six centuries, was told to pack his things and leave the palace at once. Under the protection of British forces, he left Istanbul, and his cousin, Abdul Mejid, was appointed caliph. His reign would last less than two years before the position of caliph was similarly abolished.

When the Lausanne Conference convened in France on November 20, 1922, the participants presented an interesting study in contrasts. The British prime minister, David Lloyd George, was no longer in office, in part a victim of his own stubborn refusal to compromise or negotiate, a position that many feared would lead the nation back into war. At Lausanne, England was instead represented by the British foreign minister, Lord Curzon, an imposing figure who towered a full foot over the Turkish representative, Ismet Inönü. Those who underestimated Inönü, who was essentially unknown outside Turkey, were mistaken. The clever Turkish delegate was a stubborn and skillful negotiator. When Lord Curzon would begin one of his many lengthy speeches, arguing in great detail why Great Britain could not accede to Turkish demands, the partially deaf Inönü would simply turn off his hearing aid. When Curzon's speech ended, Inönü would simply return to his original demands, as if Curzon had not uttered a single objection.[43]

This proved an annoying but ultimately successful tactic. Delegations had been sent to Lausanne from England, France, Italy, Russia, Japan, Bulgaria, Rumania, Yugoslavia, Greece, and Turkey, and these were all active participants in the meetings, signing the documents that were drawn up at the conference's end. The United States sent only unofficial observers, who participated in some of the discussions but did not sign the final treaty.

When the Treaty of Lausanne was finally signed on July 24, 1923, it was a stunning victory for Turkey, a reversal of the humiliating terms of the Treaty of Sèvres and a guarantee that Turkey could once more assume a position on the international stage. Eastern Thrace was returned to Turkey. The Aegean Islands were divided; Tenedos and Imbros were granted to Turkey, the Dodecanese were given to Italy, and those remaining were granted to Greece. The Turkish Straits were to remain a demilitarized zone under international supervision until 1936, at which point Turkey would regain sovereignty over them. The frontier with Mosul (in Iraq) was left open, to be negotiated between Turkey and Great Britain at a later date. Turkey agreed to protect the rights of Armenian and Greek minorities within

Crowds cheer around a Turkish flag to celebrate the victory at Smyrna. Smyrna was given to Greece after World War I by the Treaty of Sèvres. Within 3 years it was seized by the Turks who then regained custody through the terms of the Treaty of Lausanne in 1923.

its borders and also agreed to a mandatory exchange of populations with Greece. This excluded the Greeks living in Istanbul and the Turks living in western Thrace but would still ultimately lead to the forcible relocation of 1.3 million Greeks living in Turkey and 400,000 Turks living in Greece.[44] The hated financial terms of the Treaty of Sèvres—including the capitulations and economic privileges granted to foreigners in Turkey—were also abolished.

The Treaty of Lausanne marked an astonishing turnaround in a nation's history. In 1920, the Ottoman Empire was partitioned and occupied; less than three years later, the nation of Turkey emerged from its ashes, independent and powerful enough to renegotiate terms with the Allies and win nearly everything it requested.

On October 29, 1923, the Grand National Assembly formally declared Turkey a republic. Mustafa Kemal was elected its president.

Three years after the Treaty of Lausanne was signed, Mustafa Kemal outlined the differences between the Treaty of Lausanne and the Treaty of Sèvres in a speech that lasted six days. The Treaty of Lausanne, Kemal said, marked the defeat of an attempt to destroy the Turkish nation. "It was," he said, "a political victory unequalled in the history of the Ottoman era."[45]

A FINAL LOOK

On August 10, 1920, the Treaty of Sèvres was signed. Less than three years later, it was replaced by the Treaty of Lausanne. The treaty that had attempted to carve up the Ottoman Empire left an imprint on the Middle East, however, that long outlasted the document itself.

The Treaty of Sèvres, in its attempt to carve away much of the Ottoman Empire, inspired Turkish forces to rally together, to unify to preserve their nation, and to emerge stronger and in possession of a greater stretch of territory than the treaty had initially granted them. The revolution begun with the Treaty of Sèvres would continue after the Treaty of Lausanne had made the earlier document invalid, dramatically transforming life in Turkey under the direction of Mustafa Kemal. Kemal would abolish the caliphate, forcing all members of the Ottoman royal family into exile. The religious courts, which had used sharia, or Islamic law, as the basis for their rulings, would be closed.

Kemal was determined to modernize his nation, to transform it into a country with a population of skilled workers—women as well as men—who were educated and spoke a single language. He would largely succeed. Alcohol would be legalized; women would no longer be required to wear veils; schools would be opened to all and lessons would be taught in Turkish, not Arabic or Persian, and would focus on Turkish history, not Islamic traditions. Kemal's vision—of a prosperous and powerful Turkey with a secular (rather than religious) form of government, with a unified Turkish people marked by Western laws and thought— would largely be realized. Almost single-handedly, Kemal pulled Turkey back from the brink. The empire that had lost nearly everything—its military, its territory, its prestige, and its place in world affairs—was replaced by a modern country, which held a membership in the North Atlantic Treaty Organization (NATO) and strategic partnerships with neighbors in Asia and the Middle East.

Struggles still exist within Turkey. The borders that the Treaty of Sèvres attempted to create still serve as flashpoints. Turkish attempts to create a strong national identify left little room for other groups with other cultures and languages. Kurds still call for independence, demanding the creation of an independent Kurdistan. Revolts are always brutally put down. Kurdish organizations attempting to publicize their cause have launched a series of attacks against Turkish embassies and businesses. For the 12 million Kurds still living in Turkey, the legacy of the Treaty of Sèvres and the Treaty of Lausanne has been an ongoing struggle to preserve their language, their culture, and their way of life.

CONFLICT WITH GREECE

The arbitrary borders between Turkey and Greece have remained the subject of conflict nearly a century after the Treaty of Lausanne was signed. The focus of much of the dispute has been the island of Cyprus, about 40 miles south of Turkey. Cyprus was designated a British colony, but by the 1950s its people were demanding their independence.

This independence movement involved Great Britain, Greece, and Turkey, all of whom thought that they had an important interest in the island's future. The majority of the Cyprian population speaks Greek, and evidence of Greeks on Cyprus dates back to the earliest recorded history. Greece supported Cyprian demands for independence, believing that the majority Greek population would ally an independent Cyprus closely with Greek interests.

Turkey objected to the independence movement, noting that Cyprus' proximity to Turkey meant that the island, if allied with Greece, could pose a strategic threat to Turkey. Turkey argued that Cyprus should either remain a British colony or be divided into separate Greek and Turkish regions.

On August 16, 1960, the United Nations ended the debate, announcing that Cyprus would become an independent state—with restrictions. Great Britain could maintain two military bases on the southern and eastern parts of the island. Greece and Turkey could also maintain small military units on the island and oversee their respective populations. The president of the newly independent Cyprus was to be Greek and the vice president Turkish. Each community would have its own separate court; legal matters involving both communities would require a two-judge panel.

The result of this awkward decision was increased tension between the Turkish and Greek communities on Cyprus. In July 1974, the Greek president was overthrown by a coup, and the leaders of the new Greek government announced that Cyprus must be united with Greece. Turkish forces quickly landed on Cyprus, ultimately occupying 40 percent of the island.

A war between Turkey and Greece seemed imminent. The dispute widened to include debates over territory in the Aegean Sea. The United States responded by declaring an arms embargo against Turkey, which lasted for several years. Turkey was angered by this response from the West to what it viewed as a dispute initiated by Greek aggression and soon shifted from its pro-Western policies to form alliances with other nations, including the Soviet Union and, when the Soviet Union collapsed, formed alliances with some of its former states, including the Balkans and Central Asia. Turkey was further angered when Cyprus was declared eligible for membership in the European Union in 1993, a membership that Turkey had wanted and been denied.

Turkey has shifted position in its alliances in recent years, focusing on preserving its sovereignty and the integrity of its borders. Turkey sided with the plight of the Muslim community in Bosnia, actively participating in United Nations (UN) and NATO actions in the region. Turkey also supported UN actions against Iraq in the Persian Gulf War, allowing UN and NATO troops access to its military bases. When President George W. Bush requested the use of Turkey's bases to launch attacks on Saddam Hussein in 2003, the Turkish government at first attempted to use the deal as leverage to obtain financial and military support from the United States and then reneged on the agreement, fearful of American support for Kurdish forces in Iraq and the potential unrest that would create in the Kurdish community in Turkey.

THE ARABIAN PENINSULA

The Treaty of Sèvres named the Hijaz region of the Arabian Peninsula a "free and independent state." Had Great Britain or the other allies understood the vast wealth in oil that lay beneath the sand, they might have been much more interested in reserving that territory for themselves. At the time, however, they believed that the region was little more than a vast desert populated by Bedouins and were happy to grant the areas around Mecca and Medina to Sharif Hussain for his "Arab kingdom."

Throughout the war, British representatives had attempted to negotiate with various Arab leaders, hoping to spark a revolt against the Ottoman Empire yet uncertain who best could accomplish their aim of weakening the empire and creating a new Arabian kingdom that would be friendly to British interests. In the end, they backed Sharif Hussain, granting him far less than had been (he believed) initially promised but still giving him a kingdom of his own in the Hijaz, making his oldest son, Abdullah, king of Syria and his second son, Faysal, king of Iraq.

Faysal would prove a wily and astute ruler, maintaining his kingdom in Iraq and ultimately forcing Great Britain out of his country, establishing the nation as an independent state and bringing a swift end to the mandate. His father was less successful. Sharif Hussain's kingdom was soon conquered by Abdul Aziz, another Arab leader whom the British had courted. On January 8, 1926, Abdul Aziz was named the new king of the Hijaz, incorporating the holy cities of Mecca and Medina into a vast empire that would ultimately encompass the entire Arabian

Peninsula, an empire that would prove to contain the richest source of oil in the world.

In 1932, Abdul Aziz officially bestowed a new name on his kingdom. He named the kingdom after his family, making Abdul Aziz ibn Saud the ruler of the new kingdom of Saudi Arabia. The empire that he proclaimed would become an international power and his descendants some of the wealthiest men in the world.

THE MANDATES

The countries mandated to foreign powers under the Treaty of Sèvres would ultimately force their independence. An overwhelming Western presence in Egypt, with British troops seizing Egyptian supplies and Egyptians being forcibly drafted to fight alongside the British, sparked a rise in nationalism. Egypt was successfully declared independent from Great Britain on February 28, 1922, but it would not be until 1936, when both parties signed the Anglo-Egyptian Treaty, that Egypt was formally granted political freedom and sovereignty.

In Lebanon and Syria, the French-mandated territories felt the strong weight of France's control. Martial law was declared in several regions. Sharif Hussain's son Faysal had led a revolt that declared Syria (and Palestine) independent and proclaimed Faysal the land's king. This rebellion was quickly stamped out by French forces. Faysal's brother, Abdullah, would later be given the throne.

In both Syria and Lebanon, the French administrators immediately attempted to "civilize" the regions, opening French schools that received more funding than Arabic schools and publishing French-language newspapers. France was made the official language in the courts and government offices. Still, unrest continued in both areas. In November 1936, a Franco-Lebanese Treaty of Friendship and Alliance was signed in Beirut, and the independence of Lebanon was recognized. The government in France was soon replaced, however, and the new government refused to recognize the treaty.

Strikes and riots marked the French occupation of Syria. The French continually demonstrated a misunderstanding of Syria in the policies that they adopted, and for nearly two decades the Syrians revolted against French rule. Both Syria and Lebanon fought against German forces in World War II and later joined the United Nations as charter members. As a result, the Soviet Union, China, and the United States recognized them as independent nations in 1944. At first, France landed additional troops in Beirut (in Lebanon) and shelled Damascus (in Syria), but it was ultimately forced to buckle to international pressure. French troops left Syria in April 1946 and left Lebanon in December 1946.

Lebanon's proximity to Palestine would bring additional conflict to the region. Hundreds of thousands of Palestinian refugees crossed into Lebanon from Palestine in the late 1960s and early 1970s, and Palestinian commandos based in Beirut used Lebanon as a launching point for attacks against Israeli forces, inspiring Israeli attacks against Lebanon. The country was split between those supporting the Palestinian guerrillas and those frightened by the violence that their presence in Lebanon had brought, and civil war soon followed. The civil war soon became an excuse for international involvement, with Syrians, Palestinians, and Israeli and Arab forces all swept into the conflict. For many years, Lebanon would be overrun by Syrian and Israeli forces attempting to influence this region, which formed an unsteady buffer between their two nations.

Syria, too, would become involved in the Arab-Israeli conflict, an active participant in the wars with Israel. The question of borders has remained particularly acute in this region, dating back to the days when Palestine was first designated as the site of a homeland for the Jews.

PALESTINE

The Treaty of Sèvres granted Great Britain the mandate over Palestine, and for several decades British forces policed the growing tensions between Muslim and Jewish settlers. In the aftermath of World War II, however, Great Britain found itself unable to control all the flashpoints in its empire. India and Ireland were in chaos, but the ongoing conflict between the Muslim and Jewish communities in Palestine was a particular frustration.

By May 1947, British leaders turned in despair to the United Nations, asking the international community for its assistance in resolving the dispute. The UN resolved that slightly more than 55 percent of Palestine should be granted to Jewish settlers to form a Jewish state—more than half of Palestine was to be given to less than 30 percent of the population. Hundreds of thousands of Palestinians found themselves on the Jewish side of the territory when the British evacuated on May 14, 1948.

On this same date, a declaration of independence was read in Tel Aviv, officially proclaiming the establishment of a Jewish state to be known as Israel. Less than 24 hours later, the new state was at war with armies from Egypt, Iraq, Jordan, Lebanon, and Syria.

That war would last no more than a year, but it would be followed by other wars, and a conflict between Israelis and Arabs that continues to this day. The Muslims who lived in Palestine felt close ties with Syria and Lebanon. Much of the land in northern Palestine belonged to wealthy landlords living in Beirut or Damascus who allowed local families to live on their property in exchange for farming the land.

The neighboring Arab nations felt a strong responsibility to ensure that their interests in the region were protected. The conflict went still deeper, however. These nations were determined to see that Great Britain's promise to safeguard the rights of non-Jewish citizens living in Palestine was honored. They remembered their own recent efforts to achieve independence, and they knew the importance of guaranteeing that Arab land could not be seized and turned over to Western interests. The Treaty of Sèvres had not been forgotten. Its legacy would leave violent scars on what had once been Palestine.

IRAQ

The region once known as Mesopotamia remained a British mandate until the signing of the Anglo-Iraqi Treaty of 1930, but British occupation was uneasy. King Faysal understood that he owed his kingdom to the British, but he skillfully maneuvered his country—and the British administrators—into a position in which the treaty terminating the mandate was the most acceptable solution.

With independence came new challenges. Kurdish tribes living in the north ignored Iraqi authority, refusing to be taxed and moving from one country's borders to another. They launched uprisings in Mosul and Suleimaniyah in the 1920s and early 1930s. Although some were elected to parliament, the majority of power was concentrated in the hands of the Sunni Muslims, who, although in the minority in Iraq (Shiite Muslims formed the majority of the population), dominated government and society, forming a powerful elite.

The kingdom Faysal built did not long outlast him. Power soon shifted to the office of prime minister. Iraq joined the Allied side in the war against Germany in 1943, but from that period until 1958, Iraq experienced 21 changes of prime minister, with one man often being deposed and then returning to office later.

The formation of the state of Israel sparked additional conflict. Sympathy for the Palestinian cause was high, and by March of 1950, a law was passed allowing (in fact pressuring) Jews in Iraq to renounce their Iraqi citizenship and property. Within one year, nearly all of the Jews in Iraq had left, many heading for Israel.

A revolution in 1958 resulted in the murder of both the king (Faysal's grandson) and the prime minister. A military regime seized control and proclaimed Iraq a republic. This regime was soon overthrown by members of the newly powerful Ba'th party, closely allied with Syria. The new government focused on cementing Arab unity. Power changed hands again several times, and disagreements within the Ba'th party added to the chaos.

In 1968, a revolution led by Ba'th party members seized control of Iraq and established a new government. Its leader was Ahmad Hassan al'Bakr, and he named an ambitious aide as his second in command, a young party activist named Saddam Hussein.

Hussein built alliances with many of the most powerful forces in Iraq. He used his position as head of the Ba'th party security services to torture and murder systematically anyone who might not be loyal to him, slowly filling top positions with his supporters. After 11 years, he was powerful enough to force Bakr to step down. On July 16, 1979, Saddam Hussein was sworn in as the new president of Iraq.

Under Hussein, the twisted legacy of loyalties and shifting borders defined much of life in Iraq in the late twentieth and early twenty-first centuries. Kurdish rebels were brutally wiped out, forced to flee into Turkey and Iran or exterminated by chemical weapons. A seven-year war with Iran over disputed territory left both nations on the brink of economic disaster. An invasion of Kuwait on August 2, 1990, was also sparked in part by border disputes. When the British granted Kuwait its independence in 1961, they had left some of its border areas vague. In 1990, Hussein used these arbitrary borders imposed by the British to justify his invasion of Kuwait when Kuwaiti officials refused to negotiate border disputes with him. The truth, of course, was more complex. Kuwait and the United Arab Emirates had increased oil production shortly before the invasion, causing the price per barrel of oil to drop. The result was that Iraq lost much-needed oil revenue. By invading Kuwait, Hussein had hoped to gain greater strategic access to the Persian Gulf and add its oil resources to those of Iraq, giving him control of more than 20 percent of the world's oil production.

The invasion of Kuwait brought armed intervention by an international coalition. In 2003, Iraq was again under attack by American and British forces, targeting Hussein for his purported development of biological and chemical weapons of mass destruction. The war forced Hussein from power and left Iraq in chaos. The war also sparked intense international debate, with many nations questioning the rights of the United States and Great Britain to intervene forcibly in Iraq to force a change in regime and establish a government more friendly to their own policies and interests.

ECHOES OF THE PAST

In Iraq and throughout the Middle East, these questions continue to echo. Western efforts to influence the politics of the Middle East, to shape its governments and even choose its rulers, echo the efforts of the drafters of the Treaty of Sèvres. These attempts to reshape the Middle East into a region more friendly to Western interests proved disastrously unsuccessful in the early part of the twentieth century. Their success in the twenty-first century is still uncertain. The legacy of the Treaty of Sèvres is still being written. The borders of the Middle East continue to shift as new borders marked by conflict, religious differences, and alliances and invasions emerge.

The Treaty of Sèvres marked the end of the Ottoman Empire and created new states separated by new borders. These borders, drawn by European powers to benefit their own political and economic interests, created divisions where they had not existed and forced together peoples with different beliefs and customs, labeling them a "nation."

The leaders of these nations have been forced to cope with these externally imposed boundaries, at times fighting fiercely to preserve them, at others to alter them. Western influences continue to exert great pressure on these leaders, in many cases promising intervention if a nation's policies are deemed threatening to Western interests.

In a sense, events in the Middle East have led the region full circle, back to the days of the early part of the twentieth century, when Western goods and culture collided with Islamic traditions. Conflict and war once more define the relationship between the two. Again, Western efforts to reshape the Middle East have sparked conflict; once more Western troops patrolling parts of the Middle East have been met with a rising tide of nationalism and anti-Western sentiment.

The signers of the Treaty of Sèvres expressed their hope that the treaty would lead to a "firm, just and durable Peace." Peace in the Middle East continues to prove elusive, however, a legacy of the failed effort to divide the region with arbitrary borders.

1400s	Ottoman forces begin conquest of the Middle East and parts of Europe.
1536	Ottoman Empire signs Capitulation Agreement with France.
1908	Young Turk revolution in Turkey forces formation of new government in Istanbul.
1912	Balkan Wars cost Ottoman Empire nearly all of its European territory.
1914	World War I begins. Ottoman Empire forms alliance with Germany and attacks Russia.
1915	Armenians are deported from Anatolia; many are massacred.
1916	Sykes-Picot Agreement signed.
1917	British forces capture Gaza and Baghdad. Balfour Declaration published.
1918	British forces capture Damascus. Ottoman Empire signs armistice with Allied forces on October 30. World War I ends.

1914
World War I
begins

1917
Balfour Declaration
is published

1914 1917

1916
Sykes-Picot
Agreement
is signed

1919	Paris Peace Conference begins. Greek forces land in Western Anatolia.
1920	San Remo Conference held. Treaty of Sèvres is signed on August 10. French and Armenian forces are defeated by Turkish Nationalist army.
1921	Turkish Nationalists sign treaty with Russia; Faysal becomes first king of Iraq.
1922	Great Britain signs peace treaty with Turkish Nationalists on October 11.1923—Treaty of Lausanne is signed on July 24. British forces pull out of Istanbul on October 2. The establishment of the Republic of Turkey is announced on October 29.
1924	All members of the Ottoman royal family are expelled from Turkey, and the caliphate is abolished.
1930	Anglo-Iraqi Treaty signed, bringing an end to British mandate in Iraq.
1932	Kingdom of Saudi Arabia is created.
1936	Egypt obtains sovereignty and political freedom.

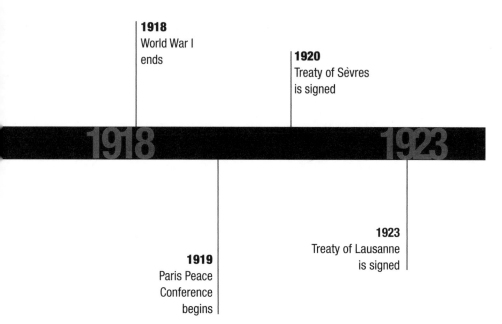

1918
World War I
ends

1920
Treaty of Sèvres
is signed

1919
Paris Peace
Conference
begins

1923
Treaty of Lausanne
is signed

1944	Syria and Lebanon are recognized as independent nations by the UN.
1946	French troops leave Syria and Lebanon.
1947	UN partitions Palestine into Jewish and Palestinian territories.
1948	British troops leave Palestine; state of Israel is declared. War breaks out between Arab and Israeli forces.
1958	Iraq is proclaimed a republic, and its king is assassinated. Civil war in Lebanon.
1960	Cyprus becomes independent state.
1967	Israel launches attack against Egypt, Syria, and Iraq.
1973	Egypt and Syria attack Israel; war lasts 16 days.
1974	Turkish forces invade Cyprus.
1980	Iran-Iraq War begins.
1982	Israel invades Lebanon.
1984	Kurdish separatists launch attacks against Turkish forces.
1987	Palestinian *intifada* (resistance movement) begins.
1988	Iraqi President Saddam Hussein launches chemical attack against Kurds.
1990	Iraq invades Kuwait.
1991	Gulf War begins.
2000	Second Palestinian intifada begins.
2003	American and British forces attack Iraq.

Chapter 1

1. Rohan Butler and J.P.T. Bury, eds., *Documents on British Foreign Policy 1919–1939*, First series, Vol. 7: 1920. London: Her Majesty's Stationery Office, 1958, p. 2.
2. Ibid., p. 4.
3. Ibid., p. 7.
4. Ibid., p. 46.
5. Ibid., p. 55.
6. Ibid., pp. 55–56.
7. Ibid., p. 231.
8. Ibid., p. 276.
9. Andrew Mango, *Atatürk*, New York: The Overlook Press, 1999, p. 219.

Chapter 2

10. Bernard Lewis, *The Middle East*. New York: Scribner, 1995, p. 219.
11. Ibid., p. 110.
12. Ibid., p. 277
13. Sidney N. Fisher and William Ochsenwald, *The Middle East*. 4th ed. New York: McGraw-Hill, 1990, p. 329.

Chapter 3

14. Ibid., p. 389.
15. William L. Cleveland, *A History of the Modern Middle East*. Boulder, CO: Westview Press, 1994, p. 153.
16. Quoted in David Fromkin, *A Peace to End All Peace*. New York: Avon Books, 1989, p. 297.
17. Justin McCarthy, *The Ottoman Peoples and the End of Empire*. London: Arnold Publishers, 2001, p. 121.

Chapter 4

18. Fromkin, p. 403.
19. Ibid., p. 279.

Chapter 5

20. Quoted in David McDowall, *The Kurds*. London: Minority Rights Group, 1992, p. 30.
21. Gerard Chaliand, ed., *A People Without a Country*. New York: Olive Branch Press, 1993, p. 35.

Chapter 6

22. McCarthy, *Ottoman Peoples*, p. 122.
23. David Marshall Lang, *Armenia: Cradle of Civilization*, 2nd ed. London: George Allen & Unwin, 1978, p. 23.
24. Richard G. Hovannisian, *Armenia on the Road to Independence, 1918*. Berkeley: University of California Press, 1967, p. 2.
25. Robert Melson, *Revolution and Genocide*. Chicago: University of Chicago Press, 1992, p. 47.
26. Quoted in Mim Kemâl Öke, *The Armenian Question, 1914–1923*. Oxford, United Kingdom: K. Rustem & Brother, 1988, p. 134.
27. Ibid., pp. 150–151.

Chapter 7

28. Don Peretz, *The Arab-Israeli Dispute*. New York: Facts on File, 1996, p. 13.
29. Ibid., p. 35.
30. <www.cia.gov/cia/publications/factbook>
31. Charles D. Smith, *Palestine and the Arab-Israeli Conflict*. Boston: Bedford/St. Martin's, 2001, p. 2.
32. Ibid.
33. Dan Cohn-Sherbok and Dawoud El-Alami, *The Palestine-Israeli Conflict*. Oxford, United Kingdom: Oneworld Publications, 2001, p. 96.
34. Ibid.
35. Smith, *Palestine*, p. 96.
36. Ibid., p. 83.

Chapter 8

37. McCarthy, *Ottoman Peoples*, p. 124.
38. Ibid., p. 125.
39. Ibid., p. 135.
40. David Lloyd George, *Memoirs of the Peace Conference*, Vol. 1. New Haven, CT: Yale University Press, 1939, p. 1.
41. Robert Lansing, *The Peace Negotiations: A Personal Narrative*. Boston: Houghton Mifflin, 1921, pp. 155–156.
42. Ibid., p. 158.

Chapter 9

43. Cleveland, *History*, p. 167.
44. Ibid.
45. Mango, *Atatürk*, p. 388.

BOOKS

Anderson, M.S. *The Eastern Question, 1774–1923.* New York: St. Martin's Press, 1966.

Butler, Rohan, and J.P.T. Bury, eds. *Documents on British Foreign Policy 1919–1939,* First series, Volume 7: 1920. London: Her Majesty's Stationery Office, 1958.

Chaliand, Gerard. *The Kurdish Tragedy.* Atlantic Highlands, NJ: Zed Books, 1994.

Chaliand, Gerard, ed. *A People without a Country.* New York: Olive Branch Press, 1993.

Cleveland, William L. *A History of the Modern Middle East.* Boulder, CO: Westview Press, 1994.

Cohn-Sherbok, Dan, and Dawoud El-Alami. *The Palestine-Israeli Conflict.* Oxford, United Kingdom: Oneworld Publications, 2001.

Fisher, Sydney N., and William Ochsenwald. *The Middle East: A History,* 4th ed. New York: McGraw-Hill, 1990.

Fromkin, David. *A Peace to End All Peace.* New York: Avon Books, 1989.

Gilbert, Martin. *Winston S. Churchill, Vol. 4: 1916–1922, The Stricken World.* Boston: Houghton Mifflin, 1975.

Hovannisian, Richard G. *Armenia on the Road to Independence, 1918.* Berkeley: University of California Press, 1967.

Huth, Paul K. *Standing Your Ground: Territorial Disputes and International Conflict.* Ann Arbor: The University of Michigan Press, 1996.

Israel, Fred L., ed. *Major Peace Treaties of Modern History, 1648–1967, Vol. III.* Philadelphia: Chelsea House, 2002.

Kedourie, Elie. *England and the Middle East: The Destruction of the Ottoman Empire, 1914–1921.* Boulder, CO: Westview Press, 1987.

Kinnane, Derk. *The Kurds and Kurdistan.* New York: Oxford University Press, 1970.

Kinross, Lord. *Atatürk: The Rebirth of a Nation.* London: Weidenfeld and Nicolson, 1964.

Klieman, Aaron S. *Foundations of British Policy in the Arab World.* Baltimore: The Johns Hopkins Press, 1970.

Land, David Marshall. *Armenia: Cradle of Civilization.* London: George Allen & Unwin, 1978.

Lansing, Robert. *The Peace Negotiations: A Personal Narrative.* Boston: Houghton Mifflin, 1921.

Lewis, Bernard. *The Middle East: A Brief History of the Last 2,000 Years.* New York: Scribner, 1995.

Lloyd George, David. *Memoirs of the Peace Conference,* Vol. 1. New Haven: Yale University Press, 1939.

Mango, Andrew. *Atatürk.* New York: The Overlook Press, 1999.

Marriott, J.A.R. *The Eastern Question: An Historical Study in European Diplomacy,* 4th ed. Oxford, United Kingdom: Clarendon Press, 1963.

McCarthy, Justin. *The Ottoman Peoples and the End of Empire.* London: Arnold Publishers, 2001.

McCormick, Donald. *The Mask of Merlin.* New York: Holt, Rinehart and Winston, 1963.

McDowall, David. *The Kurds.* London: Minority Rights Group, 1992.

McDowall, David. *A Modern History of the Kurds.* New York: I.B. Tauris, 1996.

Melson, Robert. *Revolution and Genocide.* Chicago: University of Chicago Press, 1992.

Öke, Mim Kemal. *The Armenian Question, 1914–1923.* Oxford, United Kingdom: K. Rustem & Brother, 1988.

Peretz, Don. *The Arab-Israel Dispute.* New York: Facts on File, 1996.

Smith, Charles D. *Palestine and the Arab-Israeli Conflict,* 4th ed. Boston: Bedford/St. Martin's, 2001.

Suny, Ronald Grigor. *Looking Toward Ararat: Armenia in Modern History.*
Bloomington, IN: Indiana University Press, 1993.

WEB SITES

American Memory. Today in History.
www.memory.loc.gov/ammem/today/dec28.html
The Avalon Project at Yale Law School. The Sykes-Picot Agreement.
www.yale.edu/lawweb/avalon/mideast/sykes.htm
BBC Homepage.
www.bbc.co.uk
www.cia.gov/factbook/
www.lib.byu.edu/~rdh/wwi/1919/14points.html

Humphreys, R. Stephen. *Between Memory and Desire: The Middle East in a Troubled Age*. Berkeley: University of California Press, 1999.

Kinross, Lord. *The Ottoman Centuries: The Rise and Fall of the Turkish Empire*. New York: Morrow Quill, 1979.

Lewis, Bernard. *What Went Wrong: Western Impact and Middle Eastern Response*. New York: Oxford University Press, 2002.

Mango, Andrew. *Atatürk*. Woodstock, NY: Overlook Press, 1999.

Miller, Donald E., and Lorna T. Miller, *Survivors: An Oral History of the Armenian Genocide*. Berkeley: University of California Press, 1993.

Wallach, Janet. *Desert Queen*. New York: Anchor Books, 1996.

page:

Frontis: Courtesy of the Library of Congress
Geography & Map Division
3: © Hulton|Archive by Getty Images
7: © Hulton|Archive by Getty Images
18: Courtesy of the Library of Congress,
LC-USZ62-77295
23: Associated Press, AP
28: © Underwood & Underwood/CORBIS

30: © Hulton-Deutsch Collection/CORBIS
42: © Bettmann/CORBIS
55: © Hulton|Archive by Getty Images
67: Courtesy of the Library of Congress,
LC-USZ62-131134
75: © Snark/Art Resource, NY
86: © Hulton|Archive by Getty Images
92: © Hulton|Archive by Getty Images

Heather Lehr Wagner is a writer and an editor. She earned an M.A. in government from the College of William and Mary and a B.A. in political science from Duke University. She is the author of more than 20 books, including several that explore the creation of the modern Middle East and the conflict between Israel and the Arab world.

George J. Mitchell served as chairman of the peace negotiations in Northern Ireland during the 1990s. Under his leadership, an historic accord, ending decades of conflict, was agreed to by the governments of Ireland and the United Kingdom and the political parties in Northern Ireland. In May 1998, the agreement was overwhelmingly endorsed by a referendum of the voters of Ireland, North and South. Senator Mitchell's leadership earned him worldwide praise and a Nobel Peace Prize nomination. He accepted his appointment to the U.S. Senate in 1980. After leaving the Senate, Senator Mitchell joined the Washington, D.C. law firm of Piper Rudnick, where he now practices law. Senator Mitchell's life and career have embodied a deep commitment to public service and he continues to be active in worldwide peace and disarmament efforts.

James I. Matray is professor of history and chair at California State University, Chico. He has published more than forty articles and book chapters on U.S.-Korean relations during and after World War II. Author of *The Reluctant Crusade: American Foreign Policy in Korea, 1941–1950 and Japan's Emergence as a Global Power*, his most recent publication is *East Asia and the United States: An Encyclopedia of Relations Since 1784*. Matray also is international columnist for the *Donga Ilbo* in South Korea.